Beyond the Story

CHRISTINA BIEBER LAKE

Beyond the Story

AMERICAN LITERARY FICTION

AND THE LIMITS OF MATERIALISM

University of Notre Dame Press
Notre Dame, Indiana

"This Is Just to Say," by William Carlos Williams,
from *The Collected Poems: Volume I, 1909–1939,*
copyright ©1938 by New Directions Publishing Corp.
Reprinted by permission of New Directions Publishing Corp.

Published in the United States of America

Library of Congress Control Number: 2019948585

ISBN 978-0-268-10625-6 (Hardback)
ISBN 978-0-268-10628-7 (WebPDF)
ISBN 978-0-268-10627-0 (Epub)

∞ *This book is printed on acid-free paper.*

The artist, whether he knows it or not, consults God in looking at things.

—Jacques Maritain

CONTENTS

ILLUSTRATIONS

ACKNOWLEDGMENTS

Once again I am very grateful to the members of my indispensable writing group: Tiffany Eberle Kriner, Beth Felker Jones, and Nicole Mazzarella. You each inspire and encourage me more than you know. Tiffany, there is no doubt that this book is better than it would have been because of you; thank you for going the extra mile to help me with the tone and some of the other really hard stuff.

Many other readers have provided invaluable feedback at crucial times, including Jeffrey Barbeau, Jeremy Begbie, Dan Train, and the students in Jeremy's Duke Initiatives in Theology and the Arts seminar, especially Jacki Price-Linnartz. Many thanks also go to Michial Farmer, Victoria Reynolds Farmer, and Kristin Constantine. I am immensely grateful to Stephen Little and all the folks at the University of Notre Dame Press for enthusiastically backing projects like mine. It is impossible for me to imagine completing this book without the support of my husband, Steve, and the daily reminder we get from our precious Donovan that all persons are a gift from God.

Finally, I am grateful to Rachel Lies and Jake Monseth, my faithful teaching assistants. Thank you to you and to all of my students through the years who have pondered with me the relationship between theology and the art of storytelling. This book is for you.

Beyond Darwin

Traces of the storyteller cling to the story the way the
handprints of the potter cling to the clay vessel.
      —Walter Benjamin, "The Storyteller"

A few days before Christmas in 1994, three explorers stumbled on one of the greatest anthropological treasures in human history. They found a cave in southern France that had been sealed from the elements and preserved, intact, for more than 20,000 years. It had been a Paleolithic art gallery. It contains beautiful paintings of horses and rhinos and other creatures, extraordinary works of art by any measure, that are estimated to be 32,000 years old. These caves of Chauvet are carefully guarded and curated, for now that they have been exposed, their ultimate deterioration has been hastened. But they survived long enough to be recorded with the best technology our era has to offer. An experienced film team was permitted to enter, take hundreds of photos and hours of video, and put together the extraordinary documentary, *Cave of Forgotten Dreams.*

At one point in the film, Dominique Baffier, a scholar of Paleolithic culture, leads the team into one of the farthest reaches of the cave, where there is a cluster of red human handprints on a small rock wall. She explains how they know that all the prints were made by only one man: he had a slightly crooked little finger. Several other paintings deeper in the cave were made by the same man because they bear the same crooked finger mark. This man could be the oldest artist the world will ever know, and it is stunning to imagine him there, painting. He clearly had a distinctive, particular body that enabled him to make those marks on the wall. But he also had a distinctive, particular mind that was self-reflexive enough to want to leave his mark on the walls in red paint. He was not leaving something random but patterned, or at the very least, intentionally randomized; we can imagine the painter moving like a prehistoric Jackson Pollack throwing handprints on the wall. For if there is one thing that even this handprint image indicates, it is intentionality. One particular man made these handprints, and he, or someone like him, also drew images of lions, bears, and owls on the other walls for some purpose.

What best explains why these early humans chose to paint images on the walls? What best explains why we would want to see these images, even if they did not have the added attraction of being the oldest artworks we have found on the planet? Why do we say that this art, or any kind of art, is beautiful?

These questions are very old. For much of human history they have been answered in metaphysical and theological terms. Human beings create art because they yearn to express to one another the deep intelligibility and beauty of the gift of creation itself. The artist strives to re-present that beauty in a form that is itself the "flashing of intelligence on a matter intelligibly arranged."[1] But since the nineteenth century, that explanation has been challenged, and a wholly new story about humanity's artistic impulses has emerged. That story begins with Charles Darwin.

THE ART INSTINCT

It is with good reason that Daniel Dennett, in enthusiastic support, calls Darwin's theory of evolution a "dangerous idea."[2] It is dangerous because its materialist explanation for humanity's origins has implications for every arena of human thought and behavior. For example, as Darwin's theories influenced twentieth-century America, sociologists and policy makers wrestled with how to think about the nature of human nature itself, and the conflict became a dogfight. Carl Degler's *In Search of Human Nature* traces the "decline and revival" of Darwinism in American social thought. Since the theory was initially used to advance openly racist agendas like those of Herbert Spencer, it resulted in a midcentury backlash, and culture was seen as having the upper hand in human behavior. So strong was this backlash that eventually citizens and social scientists alike assumed that culture had "severed for good the linkage between human behavior and biology."[3] But an irony remained. As Degler notes, the belief that human beings have succeeded in escaping biology was still accompanied by the conviction that humans are products of Darwinian evolution. Eventually Darwin's grand narrative returned, albeit in a more domesticated form. E. O. Wilson coined the term "sociobiology" to describe the "systematic study of the biological basis of all social behavior."[4] Sociobiology may be more domesticated than social Darwinism, but it is not shy. It endeavors to gather all human behavior under the explanatory umbrella of evolutionary origins.

With the spreading of this very large umbrella, it was only a matter of time until sociobiology also began to challenge the prevailing explanations for why we paint, compose music, and tell stories. And that is where we are today. An outpouring of publications in both the scholarly and the popular realm attest to a movement toward the idea that evolutionary theory can and should be used to explain humanity's art instinct. From Ellen Dissanayake's *What Is Art For?* to Denis Dutton's *The Art Instinct* to Jonathan Gottschall's *The Storytelling Animal*, these efforts offer slightly different explanations for why storytelling began but share the same starting assumptions.[5] Since consciousness in humans evolved over millions of years to eventually become separate from that of nonhuman animals, there must be some material and adaptive explanation for the higher-level cognitive activities that humans alone perform. Somewhere along the way the earliest humans developed what philosophers call "robust first-person perspective."[6] Only human beings have this perspective, which involves a self-concept that is necessarily achieved through social and linguistic relations. Robust first-person perspective is what enables persons to identify themselves as distinct from others and to recognize that others see them as possessing the same kind of self-awareness. All of these capacities are required for a person to produce anything we would identify as art. Paintings on the wall are meaningless without the expectation of a viewer, even if only one's future self. Making music makes no sense without the capacity for someone to recognize it. Storytelling is impossible without listeners capable of understanding symbolic narration. Since we are unaware of any other species that intentionally engages in representational activity such as painting images of buffalo on cave walls, something in our environment must have sparked the change that turned human beings into, in Aristotle's term, "mimetic animals."[7]

The sociobiological story of the origin of art depends, therefore, on a thoroughly material explanation for this leap forward into self-consciousness. And with self-consciousness the accounting becomes a bit murkier. One of the more thorough approaches to the problem is Antonio Damasio's recent book, *Self Comes to Mind: Constructing the Conscious Brain*. Damasio, a neuroscientist, argues that the early human brain became better and better at responding to its environment and was eventually able to produce "that something extra, the protagonist we carry around and call self, or me, or I."[8] To his credit, Damasio does not hide the gap in his story of how the brain generated the self-consciousness required for the third stage of human cognitive development, the "autobiographical self." While of course there are evolutionary advantages to higher levels of self-awareness (including the feelings we have about what we experience, often called qualia) there is currently no explanation for how or why such self-awareness would necessarily develop.[9] Also aware of this gap, Dennett takes a slightly different approach from Damasio. He extends the logic of naturalism to conclude that our experience of first-person consciousness—of a self or a soul—is an illusion created by the brain.[10] Dennett has written several books that refer to this idea, concluding each time that science has explained consciousness and thus definitively disproven the existence of the soul.[11] Since human beings are purely material, theology and related disciplines are outmoded and irrelevant.

Of course, humanities scholars need not, and usually do not, make any claims about the nature of self-consciousness, the origins of art, or the existence of the soul. Most literary scholars in particular resist anything that smacks of biological determinism, preferring some version of social constructivism—the idea that we are products of sociolinguistic relationships—instead. Regarded in these terms, the starting assumptions available to literary scholars seem to arrange themselves as two ends of the nature versus culture argument described above, where the former argues for biological universals and the latter insists that culture constructs everything.[12] While these positions seem to be worlds apart, their starting assumptions are more similar than they are different. Both assume that human beings evolved from simple organisms to prelinguistic primates to the advanced culture makers we are today. More important, both also assume that change comes *only* from human beings adapting to their environments. The difference is that sociobiologists emphasize biological adaptations, while social constructivists believe that other forces, such as hierarchical social structures, have greater determinative power than does basic biology. The difference is how much emphasis is put on which environments and how possible it is to change the outcome by changing the environment. In either case, the explanation for why human beings tell stories is foundationally a material one. Consequently, any contemporary scholar who begins from the assumption that human beings are more than material faces an uphill battle at best.

BEYOND THE DARWINIAN STORY

This has not always been the case, of course. The assumption regarding human origins described above reflects the larger cultural trajectory that Charles Taylor traces in *A Secular Age*. Many late modern westerners no longer believe that supernatural forces—such as God—have anything to do with our origin or our current activities. Late moderns also assume that the sciences (whether social or hard) provide our chief source of reliable information about the world, and therefore resist any definitive claims that reach outside of their purview. This scientifically tinged secularism goes by a number of names, including physicalism, materialism, scientific materialism, scientific naturalism, and metaphysical naturalism. Regardless of what it is called, this demystification and depersonalization of the world is an astounding change that is still relatively new in human history. Taylor emphasizes how profound a change it has been to move from a personal order to an impersonal one, from "living in a cosmos to being included in a universe."[13] Since there is no God to ascribe value to this impersonal universe, we make our own magic, our own meaning, and our own morality. For the bioculturalist and the social constructivist alike, this need to make our own meaning is the best explanation for art, particularly the art of story. We tell stories, argues Richard Kearney, to transform the otherwise "haphazard happenings" into narrative and our otherwise merely biological lives into human ones.[14]

But is this really the whole story of why humans began to tell stories? When we assume that naturalism is true and that any alternative account of the origins of human self-consciousness is itself a construction, are we in danger of leaving something out? In a way, the ascendency of metaphysical naturalism and the evolutionary paradigm provides a clarifying simplicity by which we can approach these questions.[15] For there can be no doubt that this account clashes with classical theism's account of human experience—including our experience of storytelling. Regardless of the position taken on the mechanism of human evolution, all theistic traditions agree that God is a transcendent, unified being who created the world. God is Aristotle's unmoved mover, the being who provides the first and final cause for all other beings. Charles Taliaferro argues that the dividing line between theists and nontheists is precisely this basic. For theists, "God is a necessarily existing being whose intentional purposive power is foundational to all reality."[16] Christian theology further defines God as a personal being who created human beings who are charged with the specific purpose of becoming more like God. For Christians, the fact that God purposefully created human beings as something other explains nearly everything about us, including the fact that we cannot be thoroughly explained. As ultimately revealed in the incarnation of God in Jesus Christ, humans are embodied persons made for relationship with God and others, the chief expression of which is love.[17] First-person consciousness is not an illusion but a mystery that enables persons to be aware of the impact of their actions on others, which is what makes the concept of love meaningful. And every human life has dignity, meaning, and eternal significance, whether a particular human being displays the ability to understand these ideas or not. The arts, and especially the art of storytelling, are an expression of that dignity, meaning, and eternal significance. They are an effort to touch it.

The danger in laying metaphysical naturalism so simply next to Christian theism is that some might think that I am trying to suggest that the issues are simplistic. They certainly are not. I want to be clear from the outset that I am not trying to write an apology for God's existence, a history of Western culture's secularization, or a defense of Christian theology. Instead, I lay these accounts side by side in order to express astonishment at the extension of metaphysical naturalism into every area of human activity, especially when it amounts to the hasty dismissal of thousands of years of theological and philosophical thinking about human nature.[18] Against this narrative of secularization, I argue that metaphysical naturalism cannot explain the art of story. My specific contention is that classical theism, and in particular, incarnational Christian theism, is the best explanation for Aristotle's insight that humans are by nature storytelling animals who take pleasure in imitation. Storytelling is a theological activity because it continually affirms and reaffirms the transcendent value of personal being. Regardless of authorial intent, stories invariably activate the part of a reader's imagination that suspects that this world is neither accident nor conclusion. We continue to long for what only a theistic cosmos can offer: a meaningful existence and a meaningful death. We still believe that our lives are tales told—and attended to. The stories we share bear witness, in an act of love, to this belief, even when the storytellers themselves claim to deny it. As such, our stories inherently resist naturalistic accounts of human experience.

While my argument could be extended to different genres, cultures, and periods, I am limiting this study to contemporary American fiction. I do not deny that certain kinds of stories—such as myth and genre fiction—often operate with very different purposes than the stories I treat here, but their existence does not disprove the point I am making about the kinds of stories we typically include in a category we still call "American literature." In this book I engage relevant theoretical categories such as the rise of religion, the postsecular, phenomenology, evolutionary psychology, and biocultural and other cognitive approaches to literature, but my avowed horizon is that of classical theism in general and Christian theism in particular.

Of course, this audacious argument cannot be definitively proven any more than the existence of God can be definitively proven. All theists could be as delusional as Sigmund Freud, Richard Dawkins, and

Daniel Dennett maintain that they are. To desire a meaningful, God-given existence is not to prove that existence has, in fact, been given and made meaningful by God. But that is not my purpose here. Our stories, I hope to demonstrate, rely on a conception of the person and of robust first-person perspective that cannot be accounted for by an impersonal universe. Our stories do proliferate but not at all like a virus. They grow in the environs of love, bespeaking the idea that our lives were meant to be celebrated, enjoyed, and shared with one another. Since both telling stories and reading them is most fittingly described as a loving attention to particular persons (as I hope to demonstrate), these activities point to God and are made possible by the God of love who is also most fittingly described *as* love. Love for persons is the fulcrum that moves the art of story.

BEING, CONSCIOUSNESS, BLISS

Love may seem like a strange thing to link to the art of storytelling. But it is not so strange when you break storytelling down to its most basic elements. Whatever else may motivate any particular writer, telling a story is always an act of one person pointing out something to somebody else, usually with joyful, passionate, or at least interested attention. Narrative, Richard Kearney reminds us, is a "quintessentially *communicative* act."[19] Since the majority of the stories we tell are about other persons, that act of attention makes no sense if the storyteller did not assume that the persons are worthy of the attention paid to them. Storytelling values a person *as* a person.

This is why I have loosely structured this book around three concepts related to personhood that are better explained by classical theism than they are by scientific naturalism: being, consciousness, and bliss. David Bentley Hart argues that these interdependent concepts are central to human experience.[20] Because of the unity of all things in God, argues Hart, we are conscious of the mystery and intelligibility of being. Furthermore, we are conscious that we are conscious of it, which generates bliss. The arts deliver exactly this kind of bliss. In my view, experiencing the bliss of the arts is why we need the concept of love to make sense of storytelling. Love is ec-static: it calls us to move out, to wake up to its presence all around us. It calls us, in other words, to go beyond ourselves toward others.[21] Love motivates the reaching out to tell a person's story, to be a witness to the beauty and intelligibility of any given person's life. "Love Calls us to the Things of this World," as the title of Richard Wilbur's poem tells us, and art gives us the bliss of enjoying those things.

In the first chapter I argue that storytelling and reading would be incoherent without personal being and that personal being is an irreducible part of the cosmos, not an emergent reality or an evolutionary by-product. I break down a very short story by Ernest Hemingway into the smallest possible elements only to show that those elements cannot be broken down to any smaller units than can be described by embodied personal consciousness, beginning with the uniquely human and irreducible self-consciousness, or the robust first-person perspective.[22] While certainly stories could not exist without the author's first-person perspective, they would also be incoherent if we were unable to assume the existence of similarly endowed persons that are beyond the author—the readers. All stories activate a living constellation of personal consciousnesses. Only personal consciousnesses display *intention*, and the intention in story is always trained toward the particular experiences of the characters. Furthermore, the storyteller and the story reader pay joint *attention* to the particular, personal, embodied being. Since this attention almost always values the dignity of the persons depicted, it is best described as an act of love.

To demonstrate how love is the fulcrum that moves the art of story is the express purpose of my second chapter. Here I consider a story told by one of American literature's most avowedly secular writers, Philip Roth, to illustrate how much a successful novel depends on a loving valuation of personal being, a valuation that theology explains better than anything else. We write stories about particular and ordinary persons because we believe particular and ordinary persons to be important.[23] While a given writer (especially Roth) might be tempted by a solipsistic view of the universe, the act of giving life to a character constantly draws him back to the mystery of being, to the inherent beauty, dignity, and freedom of other persons and other lives. *Everyman* is one of Roth's more successful novels precisely because it submits to this idea.

The third chapter delves more pointedly into the first-person consciousness of the reader as an irreducible aspect of human experience
that is central to storytelling. As I explained above, scientific naturalism's account of consciousness relies on reducing it to brain states.
What we experience when we think we are making a free choice (for
example) is actually an illusion created by our brains for our survival
benefit. In this chapter I focus on the fiction of Lydia Davis precisely
because it is probably the closest thing to brain candy that American
literature has ever produced. Davis's work gives me occasion to engage
with some of the most fascinating new research on what happens in
our brains when we read, and to demonstrate why the scientific story
can never fully account for what happens when a reader encounters
these texts.

In the next two chapters I turn to two writers who more purposefully rely on the reader's inherent reach for explanations that go beyond
the purely material world. Although they have different faith commitments, both Flannery O'Connor and Toni Morrison see storytelling as
an inherently theological—and, indeed, incarnational—activity.[24] Their
work reveals what happens when a writer begins with that conviction.
Flannery O'Connor was, of course, a master of the grotesque, which
she employed to insist that theological understanding begins in the
body. *Wise Blood* was ahead of its time in treating what neuroscience
is now discovering. In chapter 4 I explain how evolutionary theory gets
the first part right: human understanding begins in the body. But evolutionary theory fails the moment it chooses to explain away aesthetic
experience in purely material terms. For O'Connor, aesthetic experiences are a particularly reliable gateway to the divine.

Toni Morrison has never apologized for believing that this world
is not conclusion, and *Beloved* is, perhaps, her most pointed expression of that faith. Sethe, a woman who society sees as monstrous, is
Morrison's beloved. Telling her story is an act of love. Furthermore,
through its own version of magical realism, the novel draws its power
from a premodern conception of the grotesque, an aesthetic tool that
insists that both divine love and demonic destruction are real forces in
the world.

My discussion of the grotesque provides the necessary foundation
for the final two chapters, which deal with the third term in Hart's

triad: bliss. Bliss is, as far as we know, a uniquely human phenomenon. Since it comes from experiencing "consciousness of consciousness," the pleasure we take in beauty, whether in the world or in the work of art, is a supreme example. In chapter 6 I therefore challenge a recent argument that the beauty contemporary American literature offers is necessarily a substitute for God, a kind of merely linguistic bliss, or a semitranscendent "whooshing up."[25] I argue that the haunting beauty of Cormac McCarthy's *The Road* emerges from the author's witness to the goodness he sees, in an act of love, as worthy of our urgent attention. Aesthetic beauty can never be severed from the goodness that the artist sees in the world; there is no such thing as "art for art's sake."[26] Beauty calls us to stand in awe of the wonder of being itself, and our bliss testifies to that awe.

In the final chapter I extend this reasoning into the burgeoning art form of the graphic novel, illustrating how its unique fusion of language and images provides an experience of the beauty of being that is dependent on a universe that is inherently personal, particular, and made to be valued. Two very different novels, Daniel Clowes's *Wilson* and Richard McGuire's *Here*, point to this idea. The visual arts have always instructed us to pay attention to beautiful and important things; when they merge with the novel, they direct that impulse toward the beauty and importance of each person's story, no matter how banal or ordinary. Because this is true, the imaged storytelling that comprises the graphic novel might be the artist's closest imitation of God in the act of calling creation good.

FROM THE IMAGED STORYTELLING of the contemporary graphic novel, it is a surprisingly short journey back to the caves of Chauvet. Whatever else might be said about it, the artwork in these caves was no accident. It is glorious. While *glory* is not a word that late moderns are accustomed to using, it is undeniably present in those caves. The artist with the crooked finger noticed the beauty of being in the world and he re-presented it for others to see. He left his handprints on the wall and his mark on the world. He was a glorious, and gloriously attentive, human being, and he was here.

In the second century of the Christian era, Saint Irenaeus declared that "the glory of God is a living human being."[27] If we had no inkling that particular persons are created to evince this kind of glory, our stories would look very different than they do. But we still suspect that our lives here are significant, and so our stories are as full of the glory of human beings as they are of our tragic failure to live up to that promise. We have cheered for and emulated characters in *Les Misérables*, *Pride and Prejudice*, *Their Eyes Were Watching God*, *The Lord of the Rings*, and *Huckleberry Finn*. We have pitied and derided them in *Crime and Punishment*, *The Picture of Dorian Gray*, *Heart of Darkness*, *Madame Bovary*, and *Blood Meridian*. We recognize that both *Gilead* and *Lolita*, though their protagonists are quite different, are beautiful novels. We recognize that both stories speak the truth to us *through* that beauty. Can the telling of both John Ames's and Humbert Humbert's stories be called an act of love? How can both novels be called beautiful? What is more, does the beauty in these stories matter at all? Do our stories connect to some greater story, or do they just whisper meaningless desires into the wind?

   To answer these questions we must reach, by way of story itself, beyond the story of human life as a biological accident.

CHAPTER ONE

Beyond the Author

The Storytelling Consciousness and Hemingway's Baby Shoes

*And God saw everything that he had made, and behold, it was
very good.*

—Genesis 1:31

Other-Love is writing's first name.
—Hélène Cixous

Let us return, for a moment, to the caves at Chauvet. For there we saw
not only red handprints on the wall, but the result of the artistic intention of a particular man. We will never meet this prehistoric artist. His
body has long ago disintegrated; this cave painting is all that remains
for us of his existence. But in a way, we, and many others, have met
him, and certainly he expected as much, at least from his fellow cave
dwellers. Given what we know about human consciousness, we know
that any such intentional markings make no sense without others to
see them. The likeliest reason the artist painted was to share his work
with others who he expected to gain something by viewing it. This cave
artist was not alone.

The communicative aspect of all art signals the presence of human
beings, because human beings are language animals. As much as the
highest primates have achieved in symbol acquisition and manipula-
tion, none have evidenced any penchant for what Michael Tomasello

calls "joint attentional frames," in which an image is intentionally pointed to and shared by one person with another person.[1] Since this is true of visual representation, it is much more the case for stories. Stories can never be the accidental result of an animal sitting at a typewriter. Stories are always written *by* someone and they are always written *for* others who are understood to have the same abilities.[2] This basic and irrefutable argument was advanced by Steven Knapp and Walter Benn Michaels in order to argue that it is unreasonable for literary theorists to disregard authorial intent.[3] Computers can be programmed to "write" stories, but since they do not have first-person consciousness, they cannot reasonably be said to have intended them.[4] Whatever meaning such stories can be said to have is limited by the parameters of the programmer—who is necessarily a language animal.

Whatever else can be said about storytelling, the most fundamental element is that it involves intentional language use directed at a narratable event for the purpose of communicating something. Story writing and story reading therefore also necessarily involve *engaged, personal consciousnesses*. Not a singular, authorial consciousness alone but necessarily a dynamic constellation of consciousnesses, all of which are inherently personal, embodied, and irreducibly particular. All art, and especially story, depends on a relationship between conscious persons. For any story to exist, much less to have meaning, conscious persons must be intentionally interacting with each other. There is always an I and a you and a thing—usually another you—for the I and the you to focus on. The point of this chapter is to illustrate why theology offers the most viable account of that relationship.

Consider a famous story attributed to a writer not known for his theological commitments, Ernest Hemingway. Hemingway, also not known for mincing words, apparently made a wager to fellow writers: place $10 on the table if you think that I cannot write a six-word story. They did—and Hemingway won the bet. This is the story he gave them.

For sale: baby shoes. Never worn.

Nobody knows for certain if this anecdote is true. But anyone who has tried to write a six-word story—or any story at all—will immediately understand how brilliant it is. What qualifies these six words as a story, and what does theology have to do with it?

Narratologists, with customary meticulousness, have tried to break down the most fundamental elements of what constitutes a narrative. I find David Herman's description particularly helpful in this regard. To be called a narrative, it must contain

> (i) a structured time-course of particularized events which introduces
> (ii) disruption or disequilibrium into storytellers' and interpreters' mental model of the world evoked by the narrative (whether that world is presented as actual, imagined, dreamed, etc.), conveying
> (iii) what it's like to live through that disruption, that is, the "qualia" (or felt, subjective awareness) of real or imagined consciousnesses undergoing the disruptive experience.[5]

These three points help to clarify how someone can write a logical sentence and not tell a story. For example, if I write, "There's a plum on the table," it is clearly not a story because it violates all three components. There is no story because nothing happens over any amount of time and because there is no identifiable consciousness involved in seeing the plum. If we add action, "Sally gave Jim a plum," this would count as a six-word narrative, but most people would not part with their cash for it because it violates components (ii) and (iii). The difference between my "story" about the plum and Hemingway's story is crucial to my argument. Hemingway himself explained that difference, in another context. A story must always suggest a bigger story underneath the words: "If a writer of prose knows enough about what he is writing about he may omit things that he knows and the reader, if the writer is writing truly enough, will have a feeling of those things as strongly as though the writer had stated them. The dignity of movement of the iceberg is due to only one-eighth of it being above water."[6]

The key phrase here is "dignity of movement." Hemingway's story moves with dignity not just because something happens, but because it suggests something true that he wants us to see. We *know by feel* that there is more to the story than what has surfaced in its telling, and we are drawn in. We trust the vision of the storyteller because we sense that his or her perspective is insightful. Similarly, when we view a painting or a photograph of a plum, we are invited into the artist's personal perspective of the plum, and we can see its truth thereby. But "There's a plum on the table" offers very little perspective. There is very little trace of intentionality, no reason it should be this plum or that table. It gives no truth about the plum or the viewer of the plum. "Sally gave Jim a plum" has action but lacks any significant hint as to why we are being told about these events or about these people. Even William Carlos Williams's famous refrigerator-note-cum-poem, "This Is Just to Say," is a better story than "Sally gave Jim a plum."

This Is Just to Say

I have eaten
the plums
that were in
the icebox

and which
you were probably
saving
for breakfast

Forgive me
they were delicious
so sweet
and so cold

This poem, especially when viewed as a story of sorts, is the tip of Hemingway's iceberg. It gives the outline of a relationship, of a particular person who feels comfortable enough to eat someone else's breakfast but uncomfortable enough to apologize for it. To call this refrigerator note a poem or a story may be cheeky, but it certainly emphasizes that all art works on this quotidian, personal, communicative level.

It is difficult to overemphasize the importance of personal intentionality in storytelling, even when the stories are allegorical, parabolic, mythical, or abstract. The fact that an author chooses to tell a story about persons to other persons necessarily means that there is an emotive and evaluative layer, something that goes beyond the mere facts of the narrative—beyond the story. Gregory Currie has helpfully separated this aspect of storytelling from the facts of the story by the term "framework."[7] The framework is the way that storytellers set up what they want the reader to see; it represents the feeling they want us to have in our act of "joint attention" to the story and why it is being told. A framework is part of any communicative act, from the simplest gestures to the most elaborate novels. Stories *represent* events or people, but they *express* this more emotive framework, which often works on readers subconsciously.

Furthermore, this framework is the inevitable result of what narratologists usually mean by the term "focalization." Focalization is necessarily subjective. It directs the relationship between the agent who is doing the seeing, what that agent thinks she sees, and the object itself.[8] In the baby shoes story (and indeed, most stories that are not myths), the authorial presence is the primary focalizer. He produces for us an event that is really more of a selection of a possible event, a clip from the classified ads. The primary author-focalizer, Hemingway, selects the ad. The secondary author, or the implied author in this case, is also a focalizer: he or she is the classified ad writer, whose situation it is we have been led to contemplate. He or she or they have probably lost a baby in a tragic accident, but of course that is not known either. The baby shoes could have been a lousy shower gift or factory surplus. The power of the story comes from the fact that we do not know the rest of the story, but we do know, largely because of this act of focalization and framing by both the primary and secondary authors, that there is one—and that it is worth paying attention to.

In storytelling, the author's focalization is never for herself alone. Any deliberate attempt at exceptions only proves this rule. Storytelling is an act of communication with others, and here there are at least two audiences. The first audience is fictional and implied: the reader of the classified ads. Classified ads have no meaning without a community of readers of the classifieds, in this case, people who go to the ads to look for something. The second audience is us as readers of this particular classified ad, which only makes sense once we imagine the entire set of relationships it describes. We are left with the bare bones of a narration and a lot of questions, all of them irreducibly personal and irreducibly particular to the actors in *this* story. Whose baby? What happened to the baby? What does putting up the shoes for sale say about the parents? What did the readers of the classified ads feel when they saw it? Who would buy these shoes? And so on.[9]

And these are just the questions we might ask about the *content* of the story. They do not begin to scratch the surface of the kinds of questions we ask ourselves when we read such a story. Why am I so drawn in? Why do I want to know what happened? Why do I feel a deep sadness, even when I know this story has been invented? Why do I feel like I want to hug my own child? How is it that suddenly, in one second, I am led to feel a small portion of the pain experienced by those who have lost children?

If you put all of these questions together, it becomes clear that what a successful story does at its most basic level is activate a constellation of conscious and embodied presences, presences that we call persons. The energy produced by the story is increased by the iceberg factor: the unrevealed aspects of the connections between these presences, each with their own histories, memories, experiences.

Though I develop this aspect of my argument more thoroughly later, I want to contend now that the selection of persons (not plums) always clears a much bigger space and creates a more powerful chain reaction. Persons cannot be categorized and inventoried; their stories are always bigger than any depiction of their parts. Thus Hemingway and, indeed, all storytellers are to some degree in agreement with the basic ideas of the personalists, whether they acknowledge it or not.[10] Emmanuel Mounier argues that persons cannot be explained, for to explain is "to let go of the singular, of that which is one and indivisible." A person is not something that can be broken down into characteristics. "If it were a sum-total," Mounier writes, "the items could be listed: but this is the reality whose contents *cannot be put into an inventory* (G. Marcel). If they could, it would be determined by them; but the person is self-determining and free. It is a *presence* rather than a being, a presence that is active, without limits."[11]

This fundamental, active freedom of singular and irreplaceable persons is what gives life to every story, even stories that try to prove that human beings are completely determined. No story can "let go of the singular," because stories are about particular persons. Story is not about defining characteristics or scientifically predicting outcomes but about experiencing the mystery of other lives, other experiences. Stories, especially as we conceive of them in our time, simply cannot exist without this dynamic relationship.

It is easy to get ahead of myself here. I treat the reader's and the hero's presence and personalities in later chapters, but I want to begin by describing the unique status of the authorial presence and personality, because it is this aspect of the author-reader-hero triangle that most clearly defies naturalistic accounts of human experience. Authorial presence has three aspects that are best explained theologically: it constitutes a robust first-person perspective; it is an embodied consciousness that relies on the particular and irreplaceable bodies of others; and it is a consummating consciousness. The author's focalization of the other, her attention paid to the other, is best described as an act of love, so that storytelling can never be fully explained by mechanistic theories. I take these aspects in turn.

Robust First-Person Perspective

When Michel Foucault, Roland Barthes, and others declared the death of the author, it was in order to emphasize the intertextuality of texts. "Author" becomes "author function," that is, an organizing concept that imposes unity on a text that it does not have inherently. Barthes insists that whereas we used to think about the work as if unified by a single voice, we now must think about the text as if demonically possessed. It is possessed by the marvelously chaotic variety of meanings language can have, so that "against the work, therefore, the text could well take as its motto the words of the man possessed by demons (Mark 5:9): 'My name is Legion: for we are many.'"[12] The very nature of writing, he argues, is to fight against anyone who would try to exorcise these demons and control meaning. Writing "ceaselessly posits meaning ceaselessly to evaporate it." It refuses to accept an ultimate meaning of the text or of the world as text, and thus it "liberates what may be called an anti-theological activity, an activity that is truly revolutionary since to refuse to fix meaning is, in the end, to refuse God and his hypostases—reason, science, law."[13]

Barthes's admonition to resist the temptation to fix a text's meaning is well taken. Literary studies has done well to accept that no author can or should exercise control over how her words are understood. But Barthes's desire to refuse "God and his hypostases" has also unnecessarily skewed our perspective. For as our "after theory" moment has revealed (and as phenomenologists had already warned), the reduction of the author to author function has had the awkward effect of making us forget that at its most basic level any given story originated *somewhere* within *someone's* consciousness. That we may not know whose consciousness it was (Was it really Hemingway? Was it really Shakespeare?) does not change the fact that it was spoken or written by a person or persons, not found in the stars or on a monkey's keyboard. Authorial presence, in this way, constitutes a particularly robust first-person perspective. Philosophers use this term to separate mature human self-consciousness from the rudimentary consciousness found in infants and nonhuman animals. A robust first-person perspective is available only to beings who are able to identify the "I" as an "I" whose perspective is necessarily different from the perspective of the "you." In other words, it is thinking of oneself as oneself in the first person as reflected in this comment: "I don't like your photograph of me. It makes me feel fat." To be able to think of oneself as an agent with thoughts and feelings that are separate from but similar to those of other agents requires language. Furthermore, we might say that authorial consciousness is an intentionally robust first-person perspective because it is also specifically aware of itself as indexical. It points to something for others, the readers, to see. Hemingway points to the classified ad, which itself points back (through the classified ad writer's first-person consciousness) to the story of the baby. One cannot use language, and certainly cannot tell a story, without a robust first-person perspective.[14]

Why does this matter? Because in their efforts to explain consciousness within a physicalist evolutionary framework, scientific naturalists argue that our experience of this robust first-person perspective is illusory, and is in fact merely the result of certain neurons firing in our brains. Francis Crick declares, "'You' . . . are in fact no more than the behavior of a vast assembly of nerve cells and their associated molecules." Michael Gazzaniga argues that the facts make it *"clear* that you are your brain. The neurons interconnecting in its vast network . . . —that is you." [15] In her book *Naturalism and the First-Person Perspective*, Nancy Baker explains how naturalists are able to come to this conclusion. They must "purge the data of any commitments to any first-person phenomena."[16] But Baker argues that this purging cannot be done because first-person consciousness is a primary ontological reality. A person's reports of his or her subjective experiences (qualia) cannot be reduced to a nonliving bit of data without substantially changing the nature of what is being described. Naturalistic efforts to explain away self-consciousness by describing how it is processed in the brain are not dealing with the same questions. Baker writes:

> No one doubts that there are underlying mechanisms and that they are worthy of understanding. The nonnaturalist resistance is to *supplanting* philosophical questions by empirical questions about the underlying mechanisms that make the philosophically interesting phenomenon possible—as if questions about the 1985 world-championship chess match between Kasporov and Karpov could be replaced by questions about the physics involved in the motions of little bits of wood.[17]

This is not a God-of-the-gaps argument but an argument about the fundamentally unique nature of personal experience. It makes it clear why any naturalistic explanations of storytelling ultimately fall short. Storytelling requires a robust first-person perspective, which requires language. Language requires communities, and "in the absence of communities, there would be no persons: human organisms, perhaps, but no persons, no individuals who could reflect on themselves as themselves."[18] Storytelling is perhaps the ultimate example of persons reflecting on themselves *as* themselves within a community. In a way, storytelling is always reminding us that there is an inherently personal element to the world. And, as I argue throughout this book, a personal world is better explained as the work of a personal creator than as a biological accident.

Irreducible Particularity

To talk about first-person *consciousness* this much runs the risk of implying that the consciousness is the only thing that matters, not its embodiment. But this is not the case in storytelling, which necessarily highlights a holistic view of persons. Paul Ricoeur begins his analysis of narrative identity by arguing that the category "person" is a basic particular that cannot be reduced, and the "priority given to bodies is of the highest importance for the notion of person."[19] He does so to resist Cartesian descriptions of selfhood, as if who we are is best explained by mental activity, not by our experiences in the world. Storytelling, which cannot exist without giving ultimate priority to experience, proves Ricoeur correct. In his well-known essay "The Storyteller," Walter Benjamin laments that the rise of the novel, and the book as its technology, has served to move storytelling away from the idea of wise counsel given to others in a community of listeners and toward the idea of sharing information.[20] If this is true, it is much more the case in our information age, which offers the temptation to abandon the book in favor of an even more disembodied technology. It is thus easy to see why we tend to forget the fact that the author is a particular person who has written a particular text with singular events that take place in a locatable space and time. It is also easy to forget that the inventive act of writing (or telling) this story presumes an audience, as Derek Attridge tells us, so that the creation of any particular text is also best described as an event, not a thing.[21]

But we can and should remember it. Consider again the story of the baby shoes. "For Sale: baby shoes. Never worn." The arrangement of these words in this way is singular. These six words in this order and with this exact punctuation can be reiterated, of course, even with different meanings. But the singularity of these words arranged this way still remains, and is the condition for the possibility of their repetition in a way that would be recognizable as repetition. This simple fact is recognized by our legal system, which enables writers to sue individuals who take phrases from their work and use them without attribution. That our legal system can do this points to the irreducible particularity of a given utterance—even to the absurdity of trying to coin and protect a single word like *threepeat*. When we recognize that someone somewhere (maybe Hemingway) said or wrote "For Sale: baby shoes. Never Worn," we recognize it as an utterance in place and time: what theorists call *parole*. *Parole* is opposed to the word *langue*, which refers to the abstract way that language has continuity across space and time. The conversation you had with your spouse this morning highlights the event of *parole*, whereas a mythic story handed down from generation to generation highlights the idea of *langue*. A single event of *parole* may not have a traceable origin, but that fact does not erase its particular and personal origin altogether.[22]

Regardless of the question of origin, contemporary American novels and short stories are not typically mythic, and their authors certainly do not want their origins to be forgotten or erased. In our most valued stories abstraction gives way to concrete particularity, a particularity that is always personal.[23] The focal point of the story—the protagonist or hero, in this case, the parents of the baby—even though they are not real, cannot be considered abstractly. Stepping into a particular story reifies the particular stepper, too, at least in relation to this singular story. This "becoming particular" in a story can even be seen in the famous children's book *The Dot and the Line: A Romance in Lower Mathematics*.[24] The book and film prove very simply that when put in the context of a story the dot and the line cease to be mathematical and become personal and particular, even with the sound turned off. And when they become personal and particular, we also have a personal and particular reaction to them. We can have multiple reactions when we reencounter the text, but each one is also limited to a particular body (the reader) in a particular place and time.

Tellingly, the artists who have been the most eager to challenge or defy this basic fact of storytelling have not been novelists. Usually they are abstract poets enthralled by Mallarmé, whose poetry illustrates how far the artist must move away from narrative in order to inhabit the impersonal realm of "pure poetry."[25] When fiction writers try to challenge the irreducibly personal particularity of stories, the result is usually called metafiction, which is notoriously parasitic on conventional fiction for its effects. John Barth, for example, reduces story to grammatical abstraction in "Title.": "Oh God comma I abhor self-consciousness. I despise what we have come to; I loathe our loathsome loathing, our place our time our situation, our loathsome art, this ditto necessary story. The blank of our lives. It's about over. Let the dénouement be soon and unexpected, painless if possible, quick at least, above all soon. Now now! How in the world will it ever . . ."[26] Metafiction's pleasures are therefore almost entirely intellectual, and it (ironically) makes the authorial presence even more intrusive. Its stories are exceptions that prove the rule: we do not usually read novels to play a game of Mad Libs. We read to pay attention to a particular person whose story is being told by a particular other person who is gifted in the art of storytelling. Barth's rebellion depends on it.

A Consummating Consciousness: Love for Persons

The third and most important point I want to make about the nature of authorial presence is that it is a consummating consciousness. The term comes from Mikhail Bakhtin, specifically, in his early work *Art and Answerability*.[27] Bakhtin argues that for an aesthetic event to occur, particularly if that event is a narrative, there needs to be an authorial consciousness that is clearly distinct from the consciousness of the hero. If there is only one consciousness, Bakhtin insists, there can be no aesthetic event.[28] An aesthetic consummation occurs when the author describes and empathizes with an other who is not himself and then frames the other from the outside (in the story). For Bakhtin, we cannot even see ourselves in a mirror; we see instead only "raw material" of ourselves without an author. Bakhtin argues that a person has an "absolute need for the other, for the other's seeing, remembering, gathering, and unifying self-activity—the only self-activity capable of producing his outwardly finished personality. This outward personality could not exist, if the other did not create it: aesthetic memory is *productive*—it gives birth, for the first time, to the *outward* human being on a new plane of being."[29]

The work of art already suggests that we have (and need) the eyes of another person on us. When a writer tells a story about a particular person, she participates in that logic inexorably. Furthermore, the choice to tell another person's story necessarily ascribes value to that story and dignity to that person. At the very least, the author is saying, "Look! This person is interesting! Why else would I share her story?" Since telling a story is an affair of persons engaged with one another, not individuals (in isolation) defined only by some interior trait that they possess, the storyteller at least nods toward the idea of the mystery of all persons. I am using the word *mystery* the way the personalists used it: a person cannot be summed up by a list of traits. Since storytelling inherently refuses such a reduction, it is safe to assume that the mystery of persons *in and of themselves* is the highest value. This is why it does not depend on the author or characters being in any way good. Bakhtin explains that it is on the given, particular character, even a bad one, that my *"interested* attention is riveted in aesthetic seeing," so that the bad character is "the one who, in spite of everything, is the sole center of values."[30]

It is my contention that this interested attention to the inherent dignity and mystery of persons, when it is done in a way that is truly respectful of otherness, is best described as love. The concept of person is incomplete without love, and the concept of love is incomplete without persons. Personalists like Jacques Maritain argue that being a person is a "deeper mystery" than being an individual and can only be understood when love is brought into the picture. Only persons can love, making the study of the relationship between persons and love of the highest philosophical and theological import.[31]

In short, aesthetic seeing in storytelling is best described as an act of love because of the value it places on the particular, ordinary life of the protagonist (hero) that the author is consummating—and thereby suggests that our particular lives have value, too. Stories also confirm that we can no more give our own lives that value and meaning than we can give birth to ourselves. The loving relationship between author and protagonist points to the fact that we become ourselves not by way of a solitary consciousness but by intersubjectivity within a community. For many Christian theologians and philosophers, this loving intersubjectivity is the true nature of personhood, and its logic is written into the Trinity itself. According to Colin Gunton, for example, the members of the Trinity are of one substance but known by their relationship with each other, a relationship that requires that the members be different persons.[32] It is meaningless to talk about God as an idea. God is a personal being whose existence in trinitarian relationality shows that human persons are also constituted by virtue of their relationality with one another and with God.[33] Because of this, our relationships with one another as particular persons also have the capacity to lead us back to God as the only other with the ability to hold all this difference together.

The idea that an affirming intersubjectivity is what makes personhood possible explains why Gabriel Marcel believed existentialism was inherently flawed. Jean-Paul Sartre, the famous author of *Nausea*,

failed to recognize that we can only understand ourselves by starting with the other, by moving toward the other with love. One cannot give one's own life this kind of meaning, a fact to which Sartre's
Roquentin, the protagonist of *Nausea*, eventually submits in disgust:
"a man is always a teller of tales, he lives surrounded by his stories and
the stories of others, he sees everything that happens to him through
them; and he tries to live his own life as if he were telling a story."[34]
But, Roquentin continues in despair, it does not work that way: "I
wanted the moments of my life to follow and order themselves like
those of a life remembered. You might as well try and catch time by
the tail."[35] Roquentin doesn't know what he doesn't know. He cannot
be the author of his own story, or the lover, in this actualizing way, of
his own person. In contrast, Marcel, though primarily a philosopher,
wrote fiction precisely because of his personalist and antiexistentialist
convictions. Marcel gave this line to one of his characters in order to
underscore the point that love affirms the basic value of being from a
perspective that is necessarily outside of that being: "To love a being is
to say, 'Thou, thou shalt not die.'"[36] You cannot love yourself with this
kind of love. You cannot love yourself into a self.

If Bakhtin is correct that the authorial consciousness is a consummating consciousness (dependent on outsidedness), then we are
left with the question, what about deliberately autobiographical novels? While this issue is the central concern of my chapter on Philip
Roth, I want to at least raise it here. Writing in the *Atlantic Monthly*,
Nicholas Dames identified an increasing number of contemporary
writers who seem uninterested in writing novels that strengthen our
capacity for empathy for others—something that current neuroscientific research has confirmed that novels do. Instead they write what has
been called "autofiction." They share "a ruminative first-person voice
given to self-expression more than to distinct characterization."[37] They
don't really tell stories; they share reflections. Two texts he mentions
as exemplary and influential are Chris Kraus's *I Love Dick* and Karl
Ove Knausgaard's *My Struggle*. Both writers begin with the extremely
personal—sometimes even perversely so—not in order to generate empathy but "in order to evoke the cold, impassable space between self
and other." But even if Dames is correct (and I am not sure that he
is), the work of these writers simply becomes another exception that

proves the rule. As Dames puts it, it is because the idea that novels help us to build empathy is so firmly rooted now that "some novelists at least can be relied upon to resist it." The resistance requires the well-established norm that we read to learn about other lives.[38]

If aesthetic seeing in the novel involves a consummating love for the character, then the theological connection is clear. Although naturalism can explain what is going on in the brain when we value other human persons enough to read stories about them, it is classical theism that explains *why* we do. We value our lives and the lives of others because existence itself is a good gift. A gift is not a random biological accident but an intentional blessing. Our impulse to feel grateful for our lives is best explained by the idea that creation is a gift, not by the idea that our desires are illusory, the product of some evolutionary adaptation. Charles Taliaferro thus marvels at how awkwardly naturalists try to explain away these impulses. "If we do have a natural, 'inbuilt' tendency to attribute meaning to events," he writes, "perhaps this is because there is some meaning or value to being."[39] Henri de Lubac also puts it very simply: "The world is the real work of a beneficent God and has a real value."[40] It is worth remembering that since the beginning of recorded history there has been far more assent to than dissent from this idea.

Aesthetic seeing is theological because it continually reenacts this logic. As Bakhtin explains, a story is only successful as a story when the author loves her hero this way. She is able to move "the very center of value from the hero's existence as a compelling task into his existence as a beautiful given."[41] Whether she agrees with the hero or not, whether the character is as innocent as Oliver Twist or as blameworthy as Rodion Raskolnikov, the author sees all of him and values him just the same. She loves him.

While it has been commonplace since the Romantic period to compare the artist to God as creator, I believe this is a dangerous mistake. The difference is as vital to my argument as it was to both Jacques Maritain and Mikhail Bakhtin in their efforts to explain that it is aesthetic seeing that makes a storyteller an artist, not the creation of something new. While the modern artist believes she emulates God as creator, Maritain and Bakhtin suggest that the artist emulates God as seer. God sees persons as good—not perfect or sinless—but good, because being in and of itself is good. The artist reenacts, and thereby proves again and again, the initial valuation of Genesis 1:31, "And God saw everything that he had made, and behold, it was very good." This is why Maritain argued that the artist "consults God" when she looks at things.[42] Art is a virtue of the practical intellect; the artist sees with God and participates in God's glory with what she makes. Consequently, successful works of art can be neither slavishly imitative nor idealistic. Is it possible for God the creator to see the creation in either of these ways? As Rowan Williams explains, "The artist *does* set out to change the world, but—if we can manage the paradox—to change it into itself."[43]

The artist sees the world for what it is. Her loving gaze is not afraid of evil in human beings because she does not believe it is up to her to redeem human beings. The artist's job, instead, is to pay loving attention to what God has already called good, and thereby pave the way to redemption. This idea explains the great Bakhtinian insight that "in aesthetic seeing you love a human being not because he is good, but, rather, a human being is good because you love him."[44] This idea of aesthetic seeing as an act of loving attention proves it poignancy when we remember that the opposite of love is not hate. It is indifference. Storytellers can be radical, metafictional, narcissistic, experimental, ultramodern, hyperreal, historical, didactic, dogmatic, speculative, moral, immoral. They can even be sadistic or masochistic. *What they cannot be is indifferent.*

"For sale: baby shoes. Never worn." With Hemingway as our storyteller, we begin, perhaps, to feel the pain of someone who can never be known to us but could be us. Whether Hemingway intended this story to be nihilistic, an indictment of God in allowing a baby to die, is immaterial. The story itself is an act of love for persons. And when we imaginatively enter into the lives of the parents who put the baby shoes up for sale, we, too, participate in that act.

CHAPTER TWO

Beyond the Self

Escaping Narcissism in Philip Roth's *Everyman*

*I was not at all born to produce an epoch in the sphere of lit-
erature. My business is simpler and lower: my business is
above all what every man must think about, not just myself.
My business is the soul and the durable things in life.*

—Nikolai Gogol

*I read fiction to be freed from my own suffocatingly narrow
perspective on life and to be lowered into imaginative sympathy with a fully developed narrative point of view not my
own. It's the same reason that I write.*

—Philip Roth

Nikolai Gogol's *Dead Souls* is not an easy book. We bump around in
Chichikov's troika in a seemingly endless picaresque romp around
rural Russia, meeting an array of characters. Some are rude; some are
silly; some are flippant; some are downright banal. But patient readers
receive a sweet reward. To be sure, Chichikov turns out to be a charla-
tan and a crook, purchasing serfs who have recently died on the job in
order to flip them and profit from a tax loophole. But that is only a plot
device. The real story is how Gogol aligns himself with Chichikov as
the collector of the folk that nobody else wants. He collects not only
the hardworking serfs of nineteenth-century Russia's lower and middle

classes but also the "dead souls" from every other walk of life. He collects *us*. Chichikov and Gogol love these particular souls—our souls—precisely insofar as their lives *are* banal and utterly trivial. When musing over his lists, Chichikov considers the names of "peasants who had once been really peasants, who had toiled, ploughed, got drunk, driven their carts, cheated their masters, or had simply been good peasants," and is suddenly overwhelmed with emotion: "Each of the scrawls seemed to have a special character of its own and in this way the peasants themselves acquired a character of their own. . . . Chichikov was moved and said with a sigh: 'Oh Lord, how many of you there are scrawled here! And what did you do, my dear hearts, in your day? How did you rub along?'"[1] Gogol is Chichikov. In collecting Russia's most unwanted, Gogol's talent shines. He laughs with us over the once-living-and-breathing dead souls that he redeems by his interested attention—his love.

These goals, however, are a bit different from the ones to which we have grown accustomed. James Joyce famously portrayed a young man who believes that being an artist means to escape from such provincial attachments. But Gogol is not trying to forge in the smithy of his own soul the uncreated conscience of his race. He is instead the craftsman who values the undervalued souls he represents, generating a healthy, festive laughter at their foibles. Their foibles make them human, and Gogol's attention grants them the dignity he believed that every person possesses.

This dignity-granting attention is why Flannery O'Connor, Fyodor Dostoevsky, and Vladimir Nabokov so admired Gogol. It is also why Bakhtin turned to his work repeatedly. Gogol created the ideal (precisely because not idealistic) aesthetic event. He slips inside the characters only to step outside of them again, knowing that both empathy and judgment are necessary components of aesthetic seeing. As discussed in chapter 1, Bakhtin maintained that the artist's aesthetic attention is riveted on the other, even the "bad one" who is loved and given value thereby. The most "bad one" is Chichikov himself, and his beautiful givenness is emphasized by the uselessness of his picaresque journey. Gogol is not primarily the artist as creator God, but the artist as loving other. He bestows loving attention on persons and then offers the product of that attention to his readers as a gift. Since many a reader has received this gift with pleasure, we cannot say that it has been ill given or unwanted, and indeed, the best part of it might be the ability to laugh at ourselves.

Is there any way in which the contemporary American novel, as navel-gazing as it often is, can be seen to follow Gogol's lead? To answer this question I turn to a writer whose comic vision has sometimes been compared to Gogol's: Philip Roth.[2] Roth is widely considered one of the greatest American novelists of all time—and one of the most narcissistic.[3] In 2006, when the *New York Times* asked more than a hundred writers, editors, and critics to name "the single best work of American fiction published in the last twenty-five years," six of his novels made the list.[4] Roth is also a classically liberal atheist who said, "I'm anti-religious. I find religious people hideous. I hate the religious lies. It's all a big lie"; and "when the whole world doesn't believe in God, it'll be a great place."[5] He thus provides the perfect challenge to my argument that readers turn to stories again and again precisely insofar as they confirm that individual lives have God-given meaning and value in an inherently personal universe.

To make my case I turn to a novel that has been called a "resolutely human and materialist meditation on death": *Everyman*.[6] Although Roth seems bent on depersonalizing his dying protagonist and proving that his life was only heading toward a meaningless death, the novel belies its own antitheological intentions. It is a prime example of the author-hero relationship that mirrors the loving attitude of God in calling creation good, and of valuing and protecting human freedom. In its very insistence that this protagonist is "every man" and every person is worth a novel, it escapes Roth's susceptibility to narcissism and nods toward the mystery of personality.

The Life and Death of a Male Body

Roth titled his novel *Everyman* in defiant response to the famous fifteenth-century morality play. While that play elevates humankind in its universal journey to God, Roth reduces humankind to its universal journey to the grave. By never giving his protagonist a name, Roth attempts to submerge him in what he calls "our human plight—death and

nothingness," which is the novel's central theme. To emphasize the in-
evitability of this ending, the novel begins with Everyman's funeral.
The narrator tells us that all around the state of New Jersey that day
there had been five hundred such funerals, "routine, ordinary, and except for the thirty wayward seconds furnished by the sons— . . . no
more or less interesting than any of the others."[7] As we move backward
in time and watch the story of his later years unfold, we see a man embittered by years of poor health. He thinks of himself as "nothing but
a motionless cipher angrily awaiting the blessing of an eradication that
was absolute" (88). Readers are meant, it seems, to agree with the protagonist that his body is destined to be just a box of bones. We are
meant to agree with him when he asserts that he had long known that
religion was a lie and that "there was only our bodies, born to live and
die on terms decided by the bodies that had lived and died before us"
(51). Since that is the "whole of it," Everyman decides that if he were
to write an autobiography it would be titled *The Life and Death of a
Male Body*.

Regardless of Roth's intention, *Everyman* is anything but *The
Life and Death of a Male Body*.[8] The protagonist does have a name,
even if the narrator withholds it from us. His life has not been the
life of a male animal, nor has his life been merely biologically determined by the bodies that existed before his. Instead the story begins
with funeral speeches and proceedings that immediately set this particular person's life apart from every other person's life.[9] Born in New-
ark, Everyman was an accomplished advertising executive who spent
much of his life in New York City. He has had three wives, the second of which, Phoebe, was the mother of his three children. One of
his children, Nancy, was graciously loving and attentive to the end.
His brother Howie had been very close to him when they were children, before Everyman caused their estrangement. Howie still loves his
brother, however, and his speech at the funeral is not meaningless drivel
trumped up for the benefit of the survivors. He instead paints a detailed
picture of the qualities that set his brother apart as an artist. They both
worked in their father's jewelry business, but Howie "was the conventional brother." "In me," he says, "diamonds fostered a desire to make
money" (7). For Everyman the family business became a passion. As a
child he would sit in the backroom with a drawer full of watches bro-

ken beyond repair, fiddling with them. They were not worth ten dollars altogether, says Howie, "but to his budding artist's eye, that backroom watch drawer was a treasure chest" (7). We later find that Everyman had sought to become a painter. Told through his own perspective, this effort was a joke. But through Howie's perspective, which encourages us to compare Everyman to Roth and to the narrative artist in general, the metaphor becomes central. Each artist knows by instinct that each created thing is unique. Even dead souls—broken lives—cannot and should never be simply discarded.

Whatever his intention for his pitiful protagonist, Roth's novel reveals a conventional relationship between author and hero that I have been illustrating here. While the novel parodies the medieval play, it is not fundamentally ironic. Roth loves Everyman and values his life, and it is important that his existence (like that of everyone who walks this earth) is not allegorical. His analogues in fiction are not characters from a medieval play but Louis in *Nest of Vipers* or Ivan Illych in *The Death of Ivan Illych*. That Roth refuses to make his story into an overtly didactic tale of redemption or damnation only serves this point more forcefully. Because Everyman's story has no practical use as a didactic narrative, there is simply no reason to tell it unless Roth thinks that a particular person's life is worth his loving attention. This also explains why a book that contains little more plot than that of a pathetic womanizer who ages, sickens, and dies could hold our interest for two hundred pages.[10] Roth's love for Everyman is what makes the story exceed the "life and death of a male body." In short, Roth betrays his own intentions by capturing our interest in a man we otherwise would not care about.[11]

To understand how contemporary American fiction almost always works this way, consider the term "protagonist." It comes from the Greek terms for "first combatant" and has its origins in the theater. The emphasis is on the character whose *actions*—choices—make up the story. Roth makes Everyman into a recognizable person precisely because he invests him with choices. Everyman is aware of having made very bad decisions, even while he tries (sometimes but not all the time) to construe his life as something that happened to him, as if against his will (157). When his daughter tries to convince Everyman that his life is worthwhile, he reflects on the life he could have had with Phoebe and his sons and daughter, "if only he were still with Phoebe, if only Phoebe were with him now, if only Nancy hadn't to work so hard to shore him up in the absence of a devoted wife, if only he hadn't wounded Phoebe the way that he had, if only he hadn't wronged her, if only he hadn't lied! If only she hadn't said, 'I can never trust you to be truthful again'" (107–8). While it is important to the antiepiphanic nature of this story that Everyman never seems able to learn from his mistakes, the reader sees very clearly that Everyman *has had* choices. He made his own bed and is rotting in it. He left Phoebe for the insipid younger woman, Merete, knowing all the while that his having made sex into the central idol of his existence would destroy him. Everyman's efforts to convince himself that these life choices were things that "just happened to him" are stunning. Within the first few moments of their ride together in a cab, "his thumb was in her mouth, and without his knowing it, his marriage had come under assault. The young man who started out hoping never to live two lives was about to cleave himself open with a hatchet" (110–11). He is vaguely aware—but aware nonetheless—that he is trading the vibrant presences in his life for the absence that is Merete's "little hole" (both her anus and the vapidity of her life). "Only in passing did it occur to him that it might be somewhat delusional at the age of fifty to think that he could find a hole that would substitute for everything else" (113).

Though Everyman would like to believe that these things happened to him as if he was not a free actor, the narrative itself belies him. Flannery O'Connor argued that no novelist could write if our lives are "strictly determined"—biologically or otherwise. Instead, for the genuine novelist, "it is the sudden free action, the open possibility, which he knows is the only thing capable of illuminating the picture and giving it life."[12] Living involves the freedom to make real choices, and the novel's power as a genre depends on our everyday experience of this freedom as real, not imagined. To think of one's life in narrative terms at all is to admit to the reality of those choices, and to understand that those choices have formed the life we now look back on. Because of the consummating consciousness of the author, this view of freedom is preserved, even when the novelist is committed to a deterministic universe, like Émile Zola, Stephen Crane, Thomas Hardy, and Richard Wright. Is anyone willing to argue that Caroline Meeber—

Dreiser's "Sister Carrie"—made no decisions freely?[13] Certainly her choices were limited by her upbringing, her ignorance, and her current circumstances. But if she had no choices at all, there could be no novel.

Does the freedom to act, even when that freedom is substantially limited in various ways, have inherent theological significance? Gabriel Marcel thinks so. In his *Mystery of Being*, Marcel dedicates a chapter to the notion of freedom within personhood. First, he wrests the concept of freedom away from its opposition to determinism; in reality, he argues, it "lies in a completely different plane."[14] Freedom can only be understood in relation to the rich concept of personhood that he establishes throughout, and on which this project depends. Freedom is the product of robust first-person consciousness and is bound up with it. "Ultimately, to say, 'I am free', is to say 'I am I.'"[15] Somewhat paradoxically, the choices we make in true freedom can only be reflected on after the fact, as those choices, especially in regard to responsibility to others, made us who we are. One of the ways we know we have this freedom, argues Marcel, is by the preservation of an inner dialogue that is "always bound up with the act of keeping oneself open to the other" and the responsiveness that this openness requires of us.[16] This explains why *Everyman* (or any novel, I would argue) cannot be deterministic. Roth's protagonist is not an animal caught in a behavioristic loop; he carries on this inner dialogue all the time. He is intimately aware of the choices he has made, the choices that lend coherence to the person he became. Even if a naturalist were able to prove that free will is an illusion (which is what many naturalists believe—and how would you prove this?), it would do nothing to shake our daily experience of hundreds of freely made decisions, some small, some large, and some irrevocable.

Everyman knows that he has made some very large and very bad decisions that have put him in the place he now is: a lonely man who is dying. It could have been otherwise. Like anyone would, he gets angry when he feels that his family members judge him unfairly by magnifying his faults: "You condemning little shits! Would everything be different, he asked himself, if I'd been different and done things differently? Would it all be less lonely than it is now? Of course it would! But this is what I did! I am seventy-one. This is the man I have made" (97). Ironically, Roth's *Everyman* does not stray far from the medieval morality play at all. In both the play and the novel, it is Everyman's loneliness that is emphasized the most in his journey toward death. But this is a loneliness of a person who has made certain choices, developed certain habits. The only thing that the medieval Everyman can take with him to heaven is his Good Deeds, which are judged by God. In a way, the reader is a kind of judge of Everyman, trying to see what good things do remain here, knowing that our lives are just as imperfect. Regardless, the narrative makes clear that Roth's protagonist is not a mouse or a robot but a responsible, free human person. The fact that he does not have anything to show for his life is nobody's fault but his own.

NARCISSISM AND THE NOVEL

I believe that this focus on Everyman's choices, and the narrator's reflection on his choices, shows Roth at his best as a novelist—precisely to the extent that the novel departs from Roth's notorious narcissism (even as it still clearly draws on his own experiences). While Bakhtin argues that an aesthetic event only takes place when there is adequate "outsidedness" of the author from the characters, many of Roth's novels have been too tempting occasions for him to work out his own angst about himself as a novelist, his relationships with women, and his Jewish upbringing.[17] This failure is what impelled David Foster Wallace to include him, along with Updike and Mailer, among his famous collection of G.M.N.s—Great Male Narcissists.[18] Roth, like Updike, has created dozens of radically self-absorbed male characters (too much like Roth and Updike themselves) who uncritically celebrate their narcissism and never seem to learn to love anyone. Roth's fiction can be so oppressive that Carmen Callil withdrew from the judging panel of the Man Booker International prize when they awarded the prize to Roth's final novel, *Nemesis*. Roth, she reportedly said, "goes on and on and on about the same subject in almost every single book. It's as though he's sitting on your face and you can't breathe."[19] Indeed, of all the writers I discuss in this book, Roth seems the least likely to agree with what Bakhtin said about the narrative arts—that all stories have been composed about the other, and all the tears have been shed for the other, and all the cemeteries are filled "only with others," precisely because the world is "a beautiful given."[20] If Bakhtin is correct, then Roth can love his characters only insofar as he does not make them into versions of himself in order to pursue self-vindication. In other words, to love his characters truly and not narcissistically, Roth must allow the reader to judge them fairly.

An example of a narcissistic evasion of such judgment can be seen in the pivotal 1986 novel, *The Counterlife*.[21] This novel won acclaim for its experimental form: it tells a certain version of the story only to take it back and tell a different one. The protagonist at first appears to be Nathan Zuckerman's brother Henry. In one version of events he elects to have a surgery that ends his life; in a different version, the surgery leads him to pursue a Zionist's life in Israel, and so on. But Henry is not really the protagonist, and the book is not about him. It is about Nathan as a writer and the way he constructs his own life. And that turns out (surprise!) to be a thinly veiled version of Roth as a writer. The novel ends in a kind of existentialist mocking of any person's desire for an authentic and integrated life. Nathan Zuckerman declares, "In the absence of a self, one impersonates selves, and after a while impersonates best the self that best gets one through. . . . All I can tell you with certainty is that I, for one, have no self, and that I am unwilling or unable to perpetrate upon myself the joke of a self."[22]

Roth's engagement with existentialist ideas here provides a good opening for me to suggest why some novels feel more narcissistic than others, and how *Everyman* seems to escape that trap. I do not have the space here to consider Roth's engagement with Sartrean existentialism, or to give my own take on the meanings and implications of the categories of being-in-itself (*être-en-soi*) and being-for-itself (*être-pour-soi*).[23] But it is important to my argument to note the difference between Sartrean existentialism and Christian existentialism (more accurately called personalism), which is more pronounced than most scholars recognize. For example, Gabriel Marcel, though often called an existentialist, distanced his own thought from Sartre's precisely on the issue of the I-Thou relationship, on the nature of, and conditions for, true intersubjectivity. Marcel writes that intersubjectivity is impossible for the atheistic existentialist, who, following Sartre, so markedly separates being-in-itself from being-for-itself. Sartre's being-for-itself is disembodied, lost in a self-annihilating hyperconsciousness. The separation puts the person inside a kind of prison of subjectivity, where the "I" is always in a struggle to maintain the validity and irreducibility of its own point of view. Marcel writes that this separation "makes it impossible to be open to the other, to welcome him in the deepest sense of the word, and to become at the same time more accessible to oneself."[24] For Marcel, the problem is that Sartre pins the project of attaining authenticity to the ability of the person to make his or her own self. And since this cannot be done (as we saw with Bakhtin, specifically with his notion of aesthetic seeing and outsidedness), we end up with Zuckerman's claim that one's only choice is to "impersonate best the self that best gets one through." To Sartre's insistence that "man's motto is to be a maker and to make himself and be nothing but the self he has made for himself," Marcel replies that this is an aggressive denial of the reality of being that has been conferred on us in our very existence as persons. Most of all it denies the reality that life is a gift.[25]

Roth has had a long and prolific career as a novelist. While it would be irresponsible for me to make large and decisive claims about the overall direction of his work, I would argue that many of his later novels (*American Pastoral* of 1997, for example) represent a departure from his characteristic self-indulgence.[26] *Everyman* seems to be one of these. For although certainly Everyman is another version of Roth as aging, angsty writer, Roth's consciousness of this character as an other to him is more carefully (but not perfectly) maintained. To begin with, *Everyman* has far less of Roth's usual "I-know-I-am-an-asshole-but-I know-it-so-you-can-love-me-anyway" humor and thus permits the reader to make a harsh judgment on him.[27] The more carefully maintained outsidedness also gives greater power to the novel because it opens up Everyman's personality beyond the typical suburban white male's woe-is-me plight.[28] I am not arguing that Roth intentionally subscribes to the idea of the human person as a mysterious given. Rather, I am arguing that when he steps into this truer relationship of loving outsidedness to his hero, the novel's power is better explained by the mystery of personality than it is by the eliminative naturalism that Everyman himself believes.

The first sign that *Everyman* moves in a different direction is Roth's choice of the third-person perspective. Roth typically writes in the first person (most often as Nathan Zuckerman), declaring that it provides greater intimacy with his subject.[29] While there is no inherent narcissism in the first-person perspective, Roth's choice of the third person here seems to free him and the reader to imagine Everyman as someone other from him, even though the usual biographical elements are still there. Beyond that, Everyman's own approaching death encourages him to come out of himself to contemplate his parents' death with love and without irony: "They were just bones, bones in a box, but their bones were his bones, and he stood as close to the bones as he could, as though the proximity might link him up with them and mitigate the isolation born of losing his future and reconnect him with all that had gone. For the next hour and a half, those bones were the things that mattered most" (170). Everyman's overpowering sense of isolation fills him with desire for the transcendent that clearly runs counter to his own atheism. The conflict continues, "Once he was with those bones he could not leave them, couldn't not talk to them, couldn't but listen to them when they spoke. Between him and those bones there was a great deal going on, far more than now transpired between him and those still clad in their flesh" (170). The scene evokes the question God put to Ezekiel in the land of dry bones: "Son of man, can these bones live?" (Ezekiel 37:3). But unlike Ezekiel, who answers, "Oh Lord God, you know," Roth's Everyman thinks he has the answer. He pushes against his own longing for an undeniably transcendent connection by insisting that the bones themselves are all he has: "The bones were the only solace there was to one who put no stock in an afterlife and knew without a doubt that God was a fiction and this was the only life he'd have. As young Phoebe might have put it back when they first met, it was not going too far to say that his deepest pleasure now was at the cemetery. Here alone contentment was attainable" (170–71).[30]

But the obvious fact is that the bones *aren't* just bones to him. The connection that the protagonist feels to them is real. In the very next paragraph, the narrator's reflection is notably atypical for Roth: "He did not feel as though he were playing at something. He did not feel as though he were trying to make something come true. This *was* what was true, this intensity of connection with those bones" (171). The narrator does not interfere in any way, not even to mock Everyman's desire for connection to the bones. Instead, Roth goes out of his way to differentiate him from other characters who clearly do play at something or try "to make something come true"—behavior that Zuckerman insists no one can ever escape. This authorial gentleness forces the issue of how to interpret Everyman's longing for connection to the lives of his parents. Either his desire is for something merely delusional (these are just bones in a box, and his transcendent longing is silly) or he is on to something that cannot be explained by a narrative titled *Life and Death of a Male Body*. So what, then, is the best way to explain the longing for connection that Everyman displays in this scene? What is going on between him and those bones?

Were Maritain, Mounier, and Marcel standing by to interpret this scene, they would push against Everyman's (and the narrator's) version of it. For them, Everyman feels a connection precisely because he and his parents are not primarily animals whose telos is to be bones in the ground. They are persons, and "to say that a man is a person is to say that in the depth of his being he is more a whole than a part."[31] The unity of the person as a body and a spirit is mysterious. Maritain argues that what we love when we love persons is exactly this mystery, his or her "metaphysical center," that which exceeds the "nothing but" story of materialism.[32] Mounier puts it even more strongly:

> But my body is also, to myself, a vacancy, an eye wide-open to the world in self-forgetfulness. In its inner experience the person is a presence directed towards the world and other persons, mingled among them in universal space. Other persons do not limit it, they enable it to be and to grow. The person only exists thus towards others, it only knows itself in knowing others, only finds itself in being known by them.[33]

While Roth himself would deny it, these words give us the best explanation for Everyman's experience with the bones of his parents. He is just beginning to see (perhaps) that he had lived his life for himself, only to find that life an empty hole that matches the literally empty hole of the grave. But he remembers now that his richest experiences were those directed toward other persons *as* persons, and not as objects. It is those places where he best knows himself, best sees the whole of his life, best finds himself. The other (here, his parents) becomes more real to him, real enough to imagine them replying to him.[34] The seriousness of the prose is very different from the playful repartee of *The Counterlife* and many other novels. It enters fully into a kind of desire that Roth usually laughs off.

His mother had died at eighty, his father at ninety. Aloud he said to them, "I'm seventy-one. Your boy is seventy-one." "Good. You lived," his mother replied, and his father said, "Look back and atone for what you can atone for, and make the best of what you have left."

He couldn't go. The tenderness was out of control. As was the longing for everyone to be living. And to have it all all over again. (171)

This scene is not Roth's customary mocking of the longing for domestic bliss that he identified as the pathetic core of the pastoral genre. It is a dying man's recognition of the gift that his life among living persons had been. That he cannot get it back—indeed, he dies after surgery a few days later—does not lessen the significance of his finally recognizing it as a gift. And particularly, of course, it does not eliminate the fact that this recognition is retold in an act of novelistic witness.

I recognize that I could just be giving *Everyman* the benefit of the doubt. In Roth's work the battle between the novelist's best instincts are always at war with the narcissist's worst ones, and even this novel does not fully escape the latter. In short, I think Tom Jokinen is exactly right that the drama of Roth's career was that readers kept "waiting for the character who would get it, understand life outside himself, but it never happened."[35] But it is worth noting that in the medieval play, the character named "Confession" gives Everyman the jewel of penance. It is this jewel that enables "Good Deeds" to accompany and redeem him as he goes into the grave. Roth's Everyman may be the closest any of his characters have ever come to doing penance of any kind. Everyman confesses the sin of disregard for the fullness of the gift of life. After he hears the bones speak, he feels "buoyant and indestructible" and feels again the vitality of the boy "whose slender little torpedo of an unscathed body once rode the big Atlantic waves from a hundred yards out in the wild ocean all the way in to shore" (181–82). At first it seems only the self-pitying moans of a man who cannot be eighteen again. But as he goes into the surgery we are given this quite earnest expression of an unmistakably pastoral desire, with a jewel as its central metaphor:

Daylight, he thought, penetrating everywhere, day after summer day of that daylight blazing off a living sea, an optical treasure so vast and valuable that he could have been peering through the jeweler's loupe engraved with his father's initials at the perfect, priceless planet itself—at his home, the billion-, the trillion-, the quadrillion-carat planet Earth! He went under feeling far from felled, anything but doomed, eager yet again to be fulfilled, but nonetheless, he never woke up. Cardiac arrest. He was no more, freed from being, entering into nowhere without even knowing it. Just as he'd feared from the start. (182)

There is a way in which this ending is a cheap shot: Roth gets the last word on Everyman's life. He is now "freed from being" and is "entering into nowhere without even knowing it." But Everyman's experience, and the reader's experience of this scene, is not magically erased by this judgment. Unlike the truly cheap narrative cop-out, "and then he woke up—it had all been a dream!," these judgments cannot answer the question of the ultimate meaning of Everyman's near-epiphany, in spite of the feebly comic effort to do so.

Considered phenomenologically, this ending has two aspects that push against Everyman's naturalistic interpretation of his life. First, the recovery of Everyman's vitality just before he dies underlines a point that Jean-Luc Marion, a philosopher clearly indebted to Mounier, makes about the irreducible givenness of personal being. Marion argues that when a person is in the hospital (a "region of objectification") the medicalization of her body transforms her into an object, an "animal-machine." But in exiting the hospital and making banal human choices before her death (walking around, eating, thinking about things), she recovers the personhood that was hers all along. Marion explains, "I must go through that demedicalization if I want to live out, to the end, that which ultimately qualifies me as *what I am*, without possible substitution: my death in the first person."[36] In Marion's terms, Everyman dies a good death precisely because he dies as an irreplaceably particular person and not as an object.

Second, the vitality Everyman recovers at the end of his life is the vitality of the artist, his instincts to see the earth as a beautiful given.[37] Everyman's experience is truly ecstatic. He is a person going out of himself to others, the move that Mounier sees in the word *exist* itself, a "primordial motive" that leads us to express our feelings in "mimicry or in speech."[38] It is Everyman the artist who sees the "priceless planet itself" as a valuable jewel.[39] The jewel that had been penance in the medieval play becomes here the jewel of life itself, the center of the novelist's concern here and in every story. Through his father's instrument, inscribed with his father's initials, Everyman celebrates "the quadrillion-carat planet Earth!" The planet shimmers with life and vitality, with interconnection, with personal mystery that exceeds the ability of philosophy or science to reduce or objectify it.[40] Although Roth tries to doom his character, what he succeeds in doing instead is to valorize the novelist's best instincts of love toward the infinite number of personal lives he cherishes in storytelling.

Philip Roth would probably reject my interpretation of his novel with a laugh. But in a way his entire career as a novelist has inherently endorsed it. Before his retirement, he had grown increasingly tired of people failing to understand that his characters are like him but not identical to him. That irritation comes through strongly in an interview that was conducted just as *Everyman* was about to go in print. Martin Krasnik dared to ask him where Roth ended and the characters began. Visibly annoyed, Roth replied, "I just don't understand that question. I don't read or perceive books in that way. I'm interested in the object, the . . . the thing, the story, the aesthetic jolt you get from being inside this . . . thing. Am I Roth or Zuckerman? It's all me. You know? That's what I normally say. It's all me. Nothing is me."[41]

The "aesthetic jolt" that the author gets from sharing Everyman's story with us is his ecstatic experience of the world of persons as a beautiful given. It is the same jolt that led Gogol to tell his countrymen's stories and the same jolt we get from reading them. It would be hard to say that our delight is merely voyeuristic, for to do so would imply that any tenderness or empathy we felt toward the characters was false. While the word *love* has its drawbacks, it is still the best word we have to describe the experience.

CHAPTER THREE

Beyond the Brain

Your Brain on Lydia Davis

What a strange thing it is—the human brain!
　　　　　　　　　—Gustave Flaubert

No one can assume a position toward the I and the Other that is neutral.

　　　　　　　　　—M. M. Bakhtin

"I wish I had an fMRI machine."

My students looked at each other warily. They have learned from experience not to react too quickly to the assorted ways I have tried to get their attention over the years. I have cut pages out of books, analyzed poetry while sitting on the windowsill, and wordlessly handed out Chinese finger puzzles. But I do not typically venture this far into the realm of the hard sciences. So when the day for our study of the fiction of Lydia Davis had come, I had their attention. A functional magnetic resonance imaging machine, I explained, was just what we needed. A lot of interesting new research has been devoted to studying how literature plays with our brains while it messes with our heads. It would be truly revelatory to watch how our brains respond while on Lydia Davis.

The fiction of Lydia Davis has been called experimental, postmodern, "thrillingly peculiar," and even "nearly autistic."[1] Davis's fiction pushes against conventional genre boundaries and puts a cognitive spell on readers. As such, it serves both to validate and to extend some of the newest discoveries in the neurosciences about how and why our brains respond to verbal art. Since the fiction is so cognitively rich—indeed, it seems designed to play with the brain—it is also the ideal place to pose the central question of this book. Is the fiction of Lydia Davis best explained by the materialist's thesis that consciousness is "nothing but" a product of brain states, or does it necessarily point to something about first-person consciousness that is more than material?

The title of this chapter, of course, evokes the famous television commercials from years ago that featured an egg frying in a skillet with the admonition, "This is your brain on drugs." As a genre-defying writer, Davis deliberately fries the reader's brain in any and every way she can. She prods with a stimulus and watches for reactions.[2] Her desire to demonstrate the ways fiction can fry the brain emerged not from an interest in neuroscience but probably from being a longtime reader and translator of Marcel Proust.[3] Proust's legendary recollection of his childhood through the experience of eating a madeleine has been a favorite illustration of neuroscience, earning his name a place in a few recent titles.[4] Beyond the madeleine, Proust knew that readers he never met would be reading and responding to the story of his experience, too, and that our embodied emotions would also be affected, albeit in a different way. And now neuroscience can help explain how.

THE BODY IN THE MIND

Neuroscience has revealed an inextricable link between cognition, the body, and emotion. Antonio Damasio explains the findings and their ramifications most clearly. In a chapter called "The Body in the Mind" he discusses how the brain incessantly maps stimuli it receives through all areas of the body (simply put, the senses). Information from the world "cannot simply enter the brain directly," he argues, and

> because of this curious arrangement *the representation of the world external to the body can come into the brain only via the body itself*, namely via its surface. The body and the surrounding environment interact with each other, and the changes caused *in the*

body by that interaction are mapped in the brain. It is certainly true that the mind learns of the outside world via the brain, but it is equally true that the brain can be informed only via the body.[5]

The body is the means by which we interact with the world, and there is no way around it. We now know that we must modify Jacques Derrida for the twenty-first century: Il n'y a pas du hors-*chair*.[6] The body-in-the-mind discovery has motivated certain veins of literary studies for at least twenty-five years. Mark Johnson and George Lakoff were among the first to help us to understand that metaphor is itself grounded in the mind-body link through embodied mini-stories they call "image schemas."[7] Mark Turner extended their reasoning to argue that we think in parables: we are always metaphorically mapping one story onto another story, starting with the most basic stories of how we act in the world. For example, the fact that we experience events as action (one of our core image schemas) leads us inevitably to narrate our world a certain way. We might write, "The telephone pole crushed the car," even though the pole itself could not take any action.[8]

In short, whereas at one time it seemed possible to separate cognition from the body and from emotion (usually to the devaluation of emotions and the body), neuroscience has definitively disproven that effort as a Cartesian fantasy. Damasio separates the terms "emotion" from "feeling" in order to make it clear that emotions are experienced in the body first, primarily through nonconscious cognition, and then in the conscious centers of the brain. Feeling is an interpretation that the whole person makes of the experience. "While emotions are actions accompanied by ideas and certain modes of thinking," he argues, "emotional feelings are mostly perceptions of what our bodies do during the emoting, along with perceptions of our state of mind during that same period of time."[9] Damasio explains that nonhuman animals also experience emotions but lack the capacity to self-reflexively feel the emotions as such. Take, for example, a situation that would provoke fear in any conscious creature: being charged by a lion. In a human, cortisol is excreted by endocrine glands and by subcortical nuclei and is then sent to both the brain and the body, and immediate action is taken by the body (freezing up or running away). Human beings then *feel* fear, which leads them to perform other actions, such as making plans based on memories of similar events. The whole cycle starts in the brain with the perception of the stimulus that causes the fear (whether live or remembered), moves through the body in the ways stated above, and ends in different regions of the brain, where the experience is then felt. Some of those regions of the brain are connected to language, some to movement, and some to reasoning.

While the specifics of this cycle may seem complicated, the upshot is quite simple. We experience emotion through our brains and with our bodies. Even if the stimulus is not "real" (say, we read a story or watch a scene featuring a lion attacking someone), the *experience* is real and causes a reaction. The implications for literary study are clear. We have more evidence than ever of the bodily bases of the variety of approaches gathered under the heading of reader-response theory. Since literary theory began in earnest with Aristotle's *Poetics*, it is safe to say that this is something that literary scholars have always known.[10]

Lydia Davis's fiction explores and validates a variety of different aspects of these body-brain-emotions feedback loops. Her aptly named collection *Varieties of Disturbance* seems bent on reminding the reader of these connections.[11] When we open the collection, we submit to a stimulus that moves us in ways we cannot completely control. The most obvious of these experiments is "Getting to Know Your Body," which consists of two sentences:

> If your eyeballs move, this means that you're thinking, or about to start thinking.
> If you don't want to be thinking at this particular moment, try to keep your eyeballs still. (66)

Many of my students find this as invasive as it is funny. Written in the second person, the piece dares you to do something that it knows you cannot possibly do. At the very least, it does not let you forget that Davis is the one providing the stimulus, and while you can certainly shut the book to stop it, that is the full extent of your control over the experience. This is reminiscent, of course, of familiar pop psychology experiments: just try to stop thinking about an ice cream cone dipped in chocolate right now. I have made you aware that I have infiltrated your personal space with this image that I wanted to give you, at least for a split second.

Many other Davis pieces also enter into the phenomenological space of this variety of mind-body disturbance. The equally brief story "Hand" points to the author's embodiment, which gives the reader an especially uncanny experience.

> Beyond the hand holding this book that I'm reading, I see another hand lying idle and slightly out of focus—my extra hand. (*Varieties* 30)

The story expects a kind of doubling to take place, one that foregrounds the immediate present of my act of reading it. I am holding this book right now, and I see my own "extra hand," too, that is just outside of the experience of reading this book but insistent on itself nonetheless. At least, when the author draws my attention to it. Again I am made aware of my vulnerable position as reader of this text and the power of the author over me once I have given her my most precious cognitive resource—my attention. With my attention also comes my emotional response, whether I like it or not.

NOVELTY AND PATTERN

The least reductive and most interesting description of literary activity from a neuroscientific perspective that I have read is Paul Armstrong's *How Literature Plays with the Brain*.[12] Armstrong explains that the brain's response to art is a very complicated thing because there is no one area of the brain that corresponds to aesthetic activity. According to Armstrong, the main theory for why art gives pleasure is that art activates neurological activity and connection across a wide network of brain functions (43, 51). Creativity in art is best explained by a well-established insight that the brain is characterized by both a need for and attraction to novelty and a corresponding need for and attraction to pattern-creating rigidity.

Armstrong then maps this discovery onto various theories about literature that have emphasized one of the two poles. Formalist theorists, such as Viktor Shklovsky, distinguish literary art from other types of prose by defamiliarization—the ability to break us out of our habitual forms of perception. Neuroscience has observed that the brain approaches stimuli as a way to learn and grow, so it is strongly drawn to the different and the novel—the unfamiliar. On the other side, structuralist critics, such as Claude Lévi-Strauss, emphasize individual works of art as fitting into a larger pattern. Likewise, neuroscientific research indicates that the brain constantly searches for patterns—gestalts—to fit the new data into.[13] What this research enables literary critics to recognize is that both the formalist and the structuralist impulse describe true things about art and our attraction to it. We need not favor one approach over the other when coming to terms with how and why we create art and enjoy it.

The fiction of Lydia Davis appears to be designed to let us watch our own brains firing in both of these ways—often simultaneously. As a whole, the collection of stories appeals to the brain's penchant for both familiarity and constancy. The reader picks it up and expects certain conventions to be met: there's a reason for these stories being together, the term "story" means something, and so on. Genre itself is best explained by the brain's penchant for schemas. But the attraction to novelty—especially that which shatters the whole tidy idea of genre itself—is equally strong, and here Davis excels. The stories are, in short, candy for the brain.

The primary way Davis shatters genre expectations is by forcing her reader to figure out what it is that we are actually reading. Each new story cuts us loose from the whole almost entirely. Although this is always the case for readers of short stories, who have to determine anew who is speaking and what the scenario is, Davis gives her readers even more game play. These stories do not have a consistent point of view, voice, audience, length, tone, or purpose. *Varieties of Disturbance* contains a story titled "We Miss You: A Study of Get-Well Letters from a Class of Fourth Graders," which turns out to be a fictional study of a fictional study. Davis took some letters from a 1950s class, read them, and created a sociologist-narrator who noted similarities and differences. The voice of the writer claims to be detached and observant, but the piece reveals that she is not and could not be. But before we reach that conclusion (or not) we are left asking, "How do I make sense of this? Why is this here? Why do I care about a bunch of fourth graders?" The questions themselves seem to be the primary point, and the reader is left with the uniquely human experience of being a person who is interested in other persons. I return to this story below.

Varieties of Disturbance also contains stories with completely un-identifiable contexts and genres. "How Shall I Mourn Them?" might be an excerpt from a personal journal—if that journal keeper was an eccentric keeper of lists:

> Shall I keep a tidy house, like L.?
> Shall I develop an unsanitary habit, like K.?
> Shall I sway from side to side a little as I walk, like C.?
> Shall I write letters to the editor, like R.?
> Shall I retire to my room often during the day, like R.? (183)

Since the entire text continues in exactly this fashion for two pages, the reader is challenged to locate the genre and purpose of this list. The novelty draws us to it; the desire for gestalts makes us work to understand what it means. To read this book is to submit to the exploitation of these simultaneous desires of our brains.

Often Davis draws the reader's attention by decontextualizing typically banal bits of writing, such as an index to a book. The story "Index Entry" reads simply: "Christian, I'm not a" (199). Since this piece is clearly not an excerpt from an actual index somewhere, it also forces the reader to figure out how relevant the information is to *us*, that is, anyone who is holding the volume of stories in hand right now. Is Davis trying to self-disclose? Is she wanting us to see this information as a kind of key to reading the book (with awareness that looking for a key is exactly what our pattern-seeking brains always do)? Furthermore, like good stand-up comedy, the defamiliarization of the banal can also make us laugh out loud, as in "Idea for a Short Documentary Film," the entire text of which reads: "Representatives of different food products manufacturers try to open their own packaging" (*Varieties* 22). In "Letter to a Frozen Pea Manufacturer" we learn that someone is "writing to you because we feel that the peas illustrated on your package of frozen peas are a most unattractive color. . . . We enjoy your peas and do not want your business to suffer. Please reconsider your art."[14]

Stretching the limits of a genre is nothing new, of course. The aptly named novel was born in the late seventeenth century out of the indeterminacy in published material between actual news reports and fabricated items.[15] William Carlos Williams pushed poetry to the limits by publishing prose as a poem, as we saw in chapter 1. Metafiction, such as John Barth's *Lost in the Funhouse*, defines itself by toying with the reader's expectations, in large part to make the reader aware of those expectations. Marcel Duchamp put a urinal on a pedestal and called it art. Although Davis's work certainly defies genre, she seems to be less interested in defiance than she is in simply providing the reader with new and disorienting stimuli. Part of the pleasure of reading the stories is in the work we must do to situate the stimuli—to see exactly what it is we are looking at. Are we supposed to think of ourselves as reading a story or listening to a stand-up comic? The jarring newness only works because of the power of the expectation of constancy, both of which have been explained, but not explained away, by neuroscience.

THEORY OF MIND

When a reader is challenged to accommodate the perspectives of the author and characters in verbal art, we have entered an area in cognitive psychology that has accounted for many recent advances in literary study: Theory of Mind, or ToM. Theory of Mind (sometimes referred to as mind reading) is the designation given to a person's ability to anticipate what another person is thinking or feeling. It is this capacity that is compromised in autistic children, a fact that is routinely revealed by the false belief test, often called the Sally-Anne test. The test involves watching a skit that features Sally and Anne playing. Sally puts a marble in a basket and leaves the room. Anne takes the marble and puts it in her pocket. Sally returns to look for her marble. The skit watchers are asked, "Where will Sally look for her marble?" The watcher who replies, "In the basket," has Theory of Mind, because she is able to "read" Sally's mind. This capacity is required for deception, explaining why autistic children often do not understand the concept of fiction, which David Lodge aptly calls a "kind of benign lie."[16] ToM is also required for persons to have empathy for others. There is mounting evidence that literary fiction, which requires more acts of mind reading from its readers than genre fiction, can improve Theory of Mind.[17]

An excellent example of how literary fiction demands advanced mind reading from its readers is Virginia Woolf's *Mrs. Dalloway*. This novel, whose narrative perspective drifts in and out of different characters who are in the process of trying to read other characters' minds, is the central focus of Lisa Zunshine's intriguing study, *Why We Read Fiction: Theory of Mind and the Novel*.[18] When it comes to forcing readers to exercise ToM, Lydia Davis is Woolf's metaphysical granddaughter. But Davis does Virginia Woolf one better, because she forces readers to read *her* mind (why is she telling us this?) as she reads the mind of her characters who are reading other characters' minds. While there are many examples in fiction of unreliable narrators that the reader must accommodate (e.g., Poe's "The Tell-Tale Heart"), it is a different bird altogether to catch your reader in the act of reading the mind of the narrator, the characters, and the author at the same time.

"Childcare" is an excellent example of how Davis accomplishes this feat of forced, multilayered mind reading. The story contains just these seven lines:

> It's his turn to take care of the baby. He is cross.
> He says, "I never get enough done."
> The baby is in a bad mood, too.
> He gives the baby a bottle of juice and sits him well back in a big armchair.
> He sits himself down in another chair and turns on the television.
> Together they watch *The Odd Couple*. (*Varieties* 33)

This is the entire story. Neither the main character, "he," nor the narrator is named. "He" is someone complaining to himself (or to the narrator?) about having to take care of the baby. While the narrator is never named and probably not present, there are tiny bits of free indirect discourse that hint that the narrator is most likely the wife and mother: "It's his turn to take care of the baby" and the description that he sits the baby "well back" in a big armchair. The narrator also wants us to know that the main character's mood is affecting the baby. But the author and her intentions get deliberately drawn into focus in two ways: first, by the selection of an ironic title, as "childcare" is not exactly what is going on here; and second, by the final irony that they are watching *The Odd Couple*, a reference to the couple that is "he" and the baby, as well as the couple that is "he" and the mother-narrator. This makes the reader very aware of every level of mind reading that is going on—including the reader's guessing at whether or not Lydia Davis is the narrator and if she is using the story as a kind of jab at her own spouse. Theory of Mind seems to be the entire point of the piece.

"Passing Wind" is another good example. This piece is a third-person omniscient narrative about a woman caught in an all too familiar ToM conundrum (do the people around me think it was me who passed gas, and how do I know what they are thinking?). The piece begins:

> She didn't know if it was him or the dog. It wasn't her. The dog was lying there on the living room rug between them, she was on the sofa, and her visitor, rather tense, was sunk deep in a low armchair, and the smell, rather gentle, came into the air. She thought at first that it was him and she was surprised, because people don't pass wind in company very often, or at least not in a noticeable way. As they went on talking, she went on thinking it was him. She felt a little sorry for him, because she thought he was embarrassed and nervous to be with her and that was why he had passed wind. (58)

What is conventional here (at least since Henry James and Virginia Woolf) is the depiction of the main character in an act of trying to read the mind of the other character. The unnamed "she" is guessing at both the question of whether or not he passed gas and, if so, what he felt about it: "she thought he was embarrassed and nervous to be with her." She also notes her own emotions along the way—"she felt a little sorry for him"—and the reader learns many things about this protagonist. We chiefly learn that she is the sort of person who notices and worries about these difficult situations. But "Passing Wind" stretches conventions by being ultra aware of the reader's position, too. We can't help but consider that the story's euphemistic title—"Passing Wind"—might reflect Davis's awareness of the breach of decorum that even telling such a story in a literary collection might be for some of her readers.

In short, this narrative is Theory of Mind on speed. The author's intentionality comes more sharply into focus.

Part of my purpose in this chapter has been to highlight and introduce readers to the insights of so-called second-generation cognitive approaches to literature. It is telling that most scholars who take a cognitive approach to literary studies operate from the view of human mental processes spelled out above; that is, they locate cognition and emotion in embodied living persons and not in an abstract model that could be compared to the input and output of a computer. One of the leading scholars in this transdisciplinary work is David Herman, whose *Storytelling and the Sciences of the Mind* revises narratology by attending to the insights of neuroscience.[19] Herman wants literary scholarship to contribute as much to neuroscience as it takes from it, and narrative is the place where this becomes possible. In his terms, narrative works two ways: by "worlding the story" and "storying the world." Worlding the story is what readers do when we interpret narrative art, and storying the world is what we do when we use fictional narratives to make sense of the world around us. Both of these moves require high-level context interpretation. Readers of literary fiction must build patterns, draw comparisons between their own experiences and the experiences of others, make sense of new data, and so on. All of this operates in the brain and through embodied emotions in the kind of feedback loop I examined above.

Herman's work is important to my argument because his interest in neuroscience led him somewhere he probably did not anticipate. While narratologists tend to view narrative construction abstractly, neuroscience has led Herman beyond the story to the messy realm of personal intention. Herman argues that readers never make sense of narratives (worlding the story) in an impersonal way. Writers and readers are at the center of storytelling activity as *persons*, not brains. Only persons have intentions, and when we read, we always try to discover them. "Storytelling practices are inextricably interlinked with ascriptions of intentions to persons," he argues.[20] When we read a narrative that has been produced by someone (as opposed to, say, finding some nondistinct scribbles on the ground), we always and inevitably ask who produced the narrative and why. We also wonder about the narrator's and characters' intentions in the same way. This may seem like an obvious observation, but Herman's foregrounding of intentionality (especially coming from a narratologist) reminds us that neurobiology cannot explain everything we need to consider when we consider storytelling.[21] It was never meant to. Brains belong to persons, and persons have intentions. Neuroscience needs narratology as much as narratology needs neuroscience.

It might be tempting to view Lydia Davis's brain candy stories as impersonal experiments on the order of putting a rat into a cage with different shapes and smells of food and seeing what it does. But Herman's work explains why we can never—and more important, should never—do so when it comes to storytelling and narrative understanding. Since the mid-twentieth-century ascendency of the New Criticism, literary scholars have been told to disregard authorial intent as irrelevant, and that bias lingers to this day.[22] But in Davis's work, because point of view, voice, audience, length, tone, and purpose are all moving targets, the question of intentionality becomes unavoidable. In fact, it is moved front and center.

Consider again "We Miss You," the story about the fourth graders. One of the longest pieces in *Varieties of Disturbance*, this vignette appears between the two very short but also relatively (!) more conventional "Childcare" and "Passing Wind." With "We Miss You" we are immediately transported into an unexpected context and left confused. When does a short story collection ever interrupt itself for a sociological analysis of letters from a fourth-grade class to a friend who is ill? But this trick of attention getting is more than just a game. It foregrounds the question of authorial intention, which forces us to remember that Davis as an author is a person who is involved in a communicative act—even if that communicative act was merely clickbait to get us to buy and read the collection. Furthermore, and especially on display here, Davis is a person who is creating a narrator who is also a person.[23] While playing tricks with our brains, she also is constantly reminding us why we read fiction in the first place: to hear and see something of interest to another person. We know that the ethos of the writer is going to be in emotional contact with our ethos, and we want that, too. Without this element, there would be no ongoing audience for stories at all.[24]

Davis makes similar moves in her later collection, *Can't and Won't*. Many of the pieces with an assumed authorial intent (I want to exercise your Theory of Mind in a fictional context familiar to you) are surrounded by other pieces whose intent has to be actively determined by the reader. There are pieces in which the narrator relates her dreams (a particularly interesting case given that most of the time people find other people's dreams uniquely boring); pieces that are fictional letters, including "Letter to a Frozen Pea Manufacturer"; stories translated from Flaubert, such as "The Funeral"; and pieces that seem to be mere description of deliberately banal things, such as "The Cows."[25] Each of these forces the reader to ask why Davis chose to include it and what we are supposed to understand or "get" from it.

Davis's foregrounding of the question of authorial intent provides the first inroad into the question of how even these bizarre fictional experiments push against the conclusion of eliminative materialism that human experience is "nothing but" a collection of brain states. As Herman showed us, ascribing intention to others is fundamental in the operation of human cognition, and stories always elicit that activity. But what explains *why* we ascribe intention in our encounters with others, whether fictional or real?

The first thing that should be noted about this question is the inability of neuroscience alone to answer it. fMRI experiments can reveal a great deal about which areas of the human brain light up in response to what stimuli, but when it comes to *how* we experience what we do (qualia) and what that means, it can reveal very little. Paul Armstrong and David Herman are thus justifiably insistent that transdisciplinarity, especially between phenomenology and neuroscience, is essential for progress in these areas.

When phenomenology and other branches of philosophy are permitted back into the conversation, the question of human consciousness and the way it figures into aesthetic experience necessarily and productively widens. The first way it widens is by permitting us to pay closer attention to the difference between consciousness and self-consciousness, which turns out to be a very large difference indeed.

Self-consciousness, as I am using the term here, is the robust first-person consciousness I described in chapter 1. The term "first person" can, of course, refer to narrative point of view. But here it means that faculty which is *necessarily always* present (even if not specifically engaged) in fiction readers, regardless of the narrative point of view of the story. Fiction would not be appealing to a being without a robust first-person consciousness. Nancy Baker has devoted her career to arguing that any account of human cognition that attempts to reduce first-person consciousness—which she calls eliminative materialism—will fail. First-person consciousness is an ontological reality and is irreducible.[26]

Although I cannot reconstruct her multivalent argument here, I will describe the central components. First, Baker explains that eliminative materialism, ontological naturalism, and scientific naturalism are all names for theories that assume that the universe is, at bottom and to its core, impersonal. To assume that the universe is impersonal is to assume a great deal. It assumes that what people experience as free will is actually an illusion of free will, that human origins are necessarily accidental, and that the difference between nonhuman animals and humans is more insignificant than it would otherwise be. Against these assumptions, Baker argues that the cognitive sciences have not been able to explain away—or naturalize—the first-person perspective. One of the reasons this is the case is the fact that there is no room within the "nothing but" scenarios for the distinction humans are able to make between thinking of oneself as oneself versus thinking of someone who happens to be oneself. This is far less abstract than it seems (and indeed, abstraction is a problem when dealing with the whole question, as I discuss below). A famous example of the distinction is John Perry's "messy shopper" example, which is a story that Lydia Davis could have concocted. A shopper sees, through a reflective device, someone he notices is spilling sugar and making a mess in the store. He follows the mess in order to inform the hapless shopper of his irresponsible behavior, when he suddenly recognizes that he is, himself, the messy shopper. He feels ashamed and immediately changes his *own* behavior in a way he would not have thought otherwise to do. He is able to pick himself out as different from others and change his behavior accordingly.[27] This is robust first-person consciousness. The messy shopper sees himself as subject and object simultaneously.

As I mentioned in chapter 1, Baker then astutely argues that what eliminative materialists do when they ignore this distinction is (in effect) change the subject. They perform a rhetorical sleight of hand that enables them, or so they insist, to shut down inquiry and "explain" consciousness. But Baker insists, as do many philosophers arguing in a similar vein, that when it comes to first-person consciousness in particular, one cannot replace philosophical questions with rhetorical moves. This is the position taken by Thomas Nagel and Alvin Plantinga, among other prominent philosophers. Even John Searle, a committed naturalist, titles one of his short expositions of this subject *The Mystery of Consciousness* in part to emphasize that consciousness is not so easily explained as Daniel Dennett and others would like.[28] Searle points out (and Baker would agree) that eliminative materialists, such as Dennett, must deny the existence of conscious states as we usually think of them.[29] Why is first-person consciousness irreducible?, Searle asks. The short answer, he writes, is that "consciousness has a first-person or subjective ontology and so cannot be reduced to anything that has third-person or objective ontology. If you try to reduce or eliminate one in favor of the other you leave something out. . . . [B]iological brains have a remarkable biological capacity to produce experiences, and these experiences only exist when they are felt by some human or animal agent."[30]

In spite of what eliminative materialists would like us to believe, when we talk about experiences that exist only when they are felt by some agent, we are necessarily talking about phenomenology, metaphysics, and theology. Regardless of the ultimate explanation, our robust first-person existence in the world produces connections between ourselves and others that move well beyond the description permitted by neurological activity in response to stimuli.

ATTENTION, INTERSUBJECTIVITY, AND THE UTTERANCE

Consider an issue of central importance in neuroscience and the question of consciousness: attention. Certainly our brains have evolved to respond to stimuli in our environment that require our response for survival. If we smell food that is good to eat or see a lion jump out of a bush, our brains respond through our bodies and insist on appropriate action. Our attention is focused on the stimuli at hand. But in beings who have a robust first-person consciousness and Theory of Mind, freedom to choose where to give our attention comes into the equation in a stunning way. One prominent neurobiologist, Daniel Siegel, considers the issue of personal attention so central that he insists that "we are our attention."[31] It is the point of this book to argue that this is nowhere made clearer than in aesthetic activity. As creators of art, we try to get—and sustain—the attention of others in a way categorically different from animals who lack a robust self-consciousness. What does that mean?

Again I think the fiction of Lydia Davis can be appealed to to help answer the question. As noted above, her fiction highlights intentionality, particularly the general intention of a personal agent (the author) to get another person (the reader) to pay attention. In so doing, Davis's fiction suggests that it is exactly in this attention that persons pay to others—receiving from them, giving to them—that the first-person consciousness is most clearly revealed. Indeed, it is impossible to imagine first-person consciousness without the existence of some sort of community involved in acts of communication. The very existence of stories and how they operate suggest that we do not stand in a room by ourselves and become robust first-person agents. Intersubjectivity is required for "me" to become an "I."[32]

When it comes to theories of communication that accommodate this kind of intersubjectivity, it is difficult to do better than the work of Bakhtin. We have already seen how his early work defined aesthetic seeing as the act of the author seeing the character as other to her, as a Thou. In his most mature essay, "Speech Genres," he took this idea more deliberately into the study of the nature of linguistic acts themselves. Bakhtin argued (against the impersonal structuralism that was carrying the day) that the essential unit of speech communication is not the word but the utterance. This is because words by themselves, even when formed into a logical sentence, do not necessarily signify that a communicative act has taken place. A monkey typing on a keyboard could accidentally come up with a coherent sentence, but it would not be an utterance.

This observation might seem basic, but it has immense implications. The first is that any given utterance is necessarily the product of a first-person perspective that is oriented to the response of another person. An utterance, in other words, requires intentionality of the sort discussed above, but it also expects that it will have a response. The moment the listener understands what he has heard or read, Bakhtin explains, "he simultaneously takes an active, responsive attitude toward it. He either agrees or disagrees with it (completely or partially), augments it, applies it, prepares for its execution, and so on."[33] Understanding an utterance grammatically is only one small facet of a reader's response to it. Bakhtin insists that the author of an utterance does not expect her idea to be duplicated in someone else's mind (as if it were an information transfer). Instead the author expects "response, agreement, sympathy, objection, execution, and so forth"—all actions that are in part dictated by the context, the genre, of the utterance (69). The spark of expression, of communication, is born in—and indeed *lives* in—a particular utterance. Language at the level of the word or the sentence does not carry this personal spark, because it does not necessitate response. Utterances always respond to other utterances, not just to the objects of those utterances (92).

This focus on the utterance forces us to foreground what most formalist approaches to literature put in the background: reader response and authorial intention. What defines an utterance as a speech genre is its conception of its addressee. This focus is why Bakhtin did not agree with those who would draw a solid line between literary utterances and common everyday utterances. They are just different genres of communication with different audiences. The genre in which the utterance appears never supersedes the utterance itself, for each utterance is "individual, unique, and unrepeatable, and herein lies its entire significance" (105). An utterance, in other words, is as unique as a fingerprint.

Of course, we can repeat any given utterance. But every time we do so, we activate a new life event for that utterance. A text is not an impersonal thing. It lives, says Bakhtin, on the "*boundary between two consciousnesses, two subjects*"; because of the inherent intersubjectivity of the utterance, even a quoted utterance is always a new utterance (106, 108; original emphasis). With these thoughts we are, of course, back to the realm of phenomenology.[34] And that is exactly the point. There is no way in which works of literary art, created as they necessarily are with intentionality by persons and for persons, can be completely understood without recourse to persons and the still mysteriously living realm of consciousness. When we return to Lydia Davis, we see that it is exactly this view of consciousness that her work highlights. [35]

"Idea for a Sign" is one stunning example. The piece is a humorous look at what happens between persons on a train. Unlike automobile commuters, the train commuter is forced to navigate other relationships and to consider how others affect them and how they affect others. The narrator's idea is that "it might help if we each wore a little sign saying in what ways we will and will not be likely to disturb other passengers, such as: Will not talk on cell phone; will not eat smelly food" (*Can't* 6). The speaker goes on to list words that should be included on the sign that she herself should carry. Her sign will reveal that she will

> sooner or later eat something, usually a sandwich, sometimes a salad or a container of rice pudding, actually two containers of rice pudding, though small ones; sandwich, almost always Swiss cheese, with in fact very little cheese, just a single slice, and lettuce and tomato, will not be noticeably smelly, at least as far as I can tell; am as tidy as I can be with the salad, but eating salad with a plastic fork is awkward and difficult; am tidy with the rice pudding, taking small bites, though when I remove the sealed top of the container it can make a loud ripping noise for just a moment. (*Can't* 6–7)

The humor comes, of course, from the disjuncture between the necessary abstraction of public signs and the impossibly long and intricately personal signs she envisions everyone carrying around. A conventional public sign like "Mind the Gap" is intended to warn everyone to look down when they step off the train. Its utterance is meant to be simple: pay attention to your surroundings! But how could a simple sign ever let other passengers know what kind of neighbor you will be on the train? Davis thus draws our attention to the similarities and differences between a sign (including a linguistic sign, or both, like STOP) and a literary utterance. A literary utterance highlights the robust first-person perspective. In Bakhtinian terms, the two utterances differ in their respective speech genres. Whereas the linguistic sign is necessarily abstract and works by way of difference between signifiers, the literary text is necessarily personal and includes much, much more than that.[36]

Davis takes precisely the kind of particular, embodied, and ordinary thing that would nauseate Sartre's Roquentin and celebrates it. It's as if to say, "Let's all laugh together at the shared rituals we have, knowing that we each have to deal with the irreplaceable particularity of the other people who are riding on the train with us. We are always with ourselves, and there is no way around it." The piece seems to scream out Nancy Baker's insistence that "persons are fundamentally different kinds of beings from anything else in the natural world."[37] A person could never be summarized in a single utterance, much less a cardboard sign.

The Superaddressee

My purpose in bringing up Bakhtin's speech genre theory is to argue that his insistence on the unrepeatability and irreducibly particular nature of utterances best explains Davis's literary experiments. That conclusion also opens up the possibility that Davis's work points to something that Bakhtin considered a necessary ramification of this view of speech genres. Since utterances are meaningful only in the space created between the intentionality of the speaker and the responsivity of the audience, they necessarily include what Bakhtin calls a "superaddressee." Because an utterance is personal, it always has an addressee. And since no utterance can be neutral or unintentional, it also presumes a superaddressee, the respondent who will (one day) get it right. Although this superaddressee takes on various ideological expressions such as God, absolute truth, the court of dispassionate human conscience, the people, the court of history, and science, the author of any utterance *always* presupposes it. Bakhtin argues that this presupposition is a "constitutive aspect of the whole utterance" and can be revealed "under deeper analysis" in the utterance.[38] Human beings *want* to be heard, and their speech cries out for a just response. For a witness.

Unfortunately (in large part due to his political situation in Soviet Russia), Bakhtin did not fully develop the idea of the superaddressee. It is safe to say that he did not intend the concept to serve as some necessary evidence of God's existence but rather as a corrective to the abstract, disembodied, and depersonalized theories of the structuralist critics of his age. An addressee can never be someone (or a collection of someones) without a robust first-person consciousness. From here, for the personalists working out the implications of the existence of robust first-person consciousness, it is a small step to theology.

Henri de Lubac is one such thinker. His work *The Discovery of God* is his effort to counter the existential atheism of his day by fleshing out Aquinas's insistence that "all knowers know God implicitly in all they know."[39] Because de Lubac knew that this axiom can never be proven, his book is an effort to explain how assuming the existence of a personal creator God makes more sense of experiences here than does Sartre's insistence that it all amounts to nothingness. He believed that knowing the reality of the world of human beings would lead one to know the reality of God. In short, if to know a human being is to recognize that she is a personal being (with all that entails), then it makes better sense to be open to the fact that there is an ultimately personal creator of that being. God is the mysterious, absolute other, the being enclosed within itself, "always beyond our grasp, the totally personal Being, 'the only *Thou* which, by definition, cannot become *That*.'"[40]

For de Lubac, the personality of God undergirds everything. His book is thus a kind of exposition of Colossians 1, which proclaims that the whole world is held together in the person of Christ. De Lubac writes that "every human act, whether it is an act of knowledge or an act of the will, rests secretly upon God, by attributing meaning and solidity to the real upon which it is exercised."[41] Water remains water even when we aren't thinking about it; likewise, it matters little whether or not human beings recognize that all their mental and physical acts rest on God. But to see the world of human being as a real, solid, and ultimately personal thing is to begin down the road toward that affirmation. There is always freedom to reject it.

Can these unabashedly theological ideas better explain our response to the work of Lydia Davis? I believe they do. Take the very short story "Lonely." Its brevity allows me to present it whole.

No one is calling me. I can't check the answering machine because I have been here all this time. If I go out, someone may call while I'm out. Then I can check the answering machine when I come back in. (*Varieties* 86)

First, recalling Bakhtin, we should note that these sentences have meaning only insofar as they are considered as an utterance that is the result of authorial purpose. As we have seen, we naturally ascribe intentionality to works of art, and the appearance of this piece in a collection subtitled "Stories" indicates how we should read it. The speaker is a character, the hero (if you will) of a narrative utterance, and we are invited to respond to the utterance and the experience it represents. It calls on us to exercise Theory of Mind as it assumes our interest in and our ability to empathize with others. We read the mind of the character by connecting his or her experience to our own similar experiences. There is no need to wonder whether or not the story is "true" because the reader immediately recognizes that it could be (and has been) true of particular individuals somewhere at some time in some way—maybe even the person reading the story at this particular moment. Second, although the attention that we are implicitly asked to pay to this individual person's story could be given because of various utilitarian motives (I want information or financial gain of some sort), those motives do not explain why Davis wrote "Lonely" or why anyone would want to read it. We give our attention to this person because the artist is giving her attention to her. We see this person (who could be me! My daughter! My neighbor!) sitting in her house waiting for phone calls that never come. We see that she is lonely. But now, because we have also become witnesses to this utterance, we also see that she is not actually alone and cannot be. Can the collective witness of the writer and the reader, in this scenario, be best explained as an act of love?

Some will object at this point that the creation of fictitious persons belies this reasoning. I think, instead, that it strengthens it. We just don't read stories (or not for very long) that work at cross purposes with the usual mode of storytelling by trying to create an impersonal gap between us and the characters.[42] We also don't read stories primarily because we like how they play with our brains. We read precisely for the personal flash of recognition of others and ourselves. We read to see and hear others because we, too, want to be seen and heard. We also suspect, deep down, that we *have been seen* our whole lives. In an interview, Davis was asked how she handles the fact that she sometimes draws on experiences of her friends in her writing. She responded:

> One friend was very uncomfortable. Another friend skimmed the story to find all the places she appeared to see if they were okay. Then she settled down and read it again from the beginning. She said it actually had a very good effect on her because at that time she was feeling: What does my life add up to? She's in her forties, and enough decades have gone by so she was feeling a little discouraged. When she saw herself in print and saw all the things that she had said and done and thought, she had a different feeling. Her life did add up to something. She was a real person. Not because she was in the book, but because the book showed her to herself.[43]

Of course, the desire to become a "real person" does not prove the existence of God as a personal superaddressee.[44] But the joy of being seen and heard is not best explained as an impersonal epiphenomenon, an illusion of self-consciousness. Our suspicion that we are not ultimately alone is best explained by a loving "Thou" who can never be "That," and who, in spite of everything, loves us enough to pay attention to us.

CHAPTER FOUR

Beyond Evolution

Flannery O'Connor's *Wise Blood* and the Language Animal

The more we really look at man as an animal, the less he will look like one.

—G. K. Chesterton

In the shock of joy in response to good art, an essential ingredient is a sense of the revelation of reality, of the really real. . . . The world as we were never able so clearly to see it before.

—Iris Murdoch

I began my teaching career shortly after the release of a Hollywood blockbuster that became the bane of my existence: *Dead Poets Society*. What English teacher could possibly be as cool as Robin Williams playing Mr. Keating? What I could not predict was that thirty years later the hippest theory of language around would also be Mr. Keating's.

> Keating: "Language was developed for one endeavor, and that is . . . ?" (*he looks around the classroom*)
> Student: (*tentatively*) "To communicate?"
> Keating: "No! To woo women!"

As we have already seen, evolutionary explanations for humanity's art instinct are currently in vogue and take a variety of forms. Since the

67

primary concern within the evolutionary paradigm is to establish the adaptive advantages created by (in this case) storytelling, some argue that sexual selection must be the real root. Like a peacock sporting a beautiful tail, a tale beautifully told by a person attracts suitors, and the genetic disposition for linguistic art thereby proliferates. Steven Pinker is a notable opponent of this explanation, favoring instead what is sometimes called the "cheesecake thesis." Art is a by-product of adaptation: humans increasingly created designs because the activity delivers cognitive sweets for the brain.[1] There are a number of other positions under this biocultural umbrella, and the only thing that they share is an aggressive metaphysical naturalism that insists that the best explanation for story is necessarily a material explanation.[2] Humans are storytelling animals—with the emphasis plainly on the animal. And the biggest story human animals ever made up is the story of God's existence.

One of the more compelling of these sociobiological accounts is *On the Origin of Stories*, by Brian Boyd, a prominent Nabokov scholar. Although Boyd does not argue that Darwinian evolution can explain everything about the art of storytelling, he does insist on an entirely naturalistic explanation for its origin and early development. He argues that the adaptive advantages of storytelling were not primarily in the area of sexual selection or even social connectivity, but were (and are) cognitive. Art is a unique kind of cognitive play that emerges from the brain's evident delight in pattern recognition. Just as sexual pleasure ensures that we survive as a species, the cognitive pleasures of storytelling ensure that we stay open to the kinds of information we need to thrive as a human community. Since humans, more than any other species, depend on information about other humans—their capacities, intentions, reactions, and so forth—we developed the capacity to anticipate what others are thinking and feeling. This is Theory of Mind. Boyd argues that ToM may even be more important than language to the expansion of the human brain.[3] Since telling imaginative stories is a good way to exercise ToM, and thereby promote the social cohesion so useful for survival, it gathers up quite nicely under a sociobiological umbrella. Religion, for example, is a fictitious product of this impulse for storytelling and exists primarily to promote social cohesion. And because these religious myths are so useful, explains Boyd, they "prove hard to dislodge despite their detachment from fact."[4]

There is, of course, more nuance to this argument, but I have tried to summarize it faithfully. While there is no reason to reject the idea that humans gain cognitive and social advantages from storytelling, I still believe that this explanation is missing something much more basic. This default to metaphysical naturalism performs a disservice by blinding us to a deeper understanding of the unique access to reality that storytelling provides. For that, as I have been insisting throughout, we will need the resources of phenomenology and theology. Although phenomenology as a philosophical enterprise encompasses quite a few different approaches, nearly all of them resist the methodological and metaphysical naturalism assumed by evolutionary explanations.[5] They do this by returning us to the most basic question of all: what is really happening when we play with language, especially when we use it to make up stories for one another? For phenomenology, adaptation accounts inevitably fail to take adequately into account the complex nature of what language is being used to describe—what it is often *about*. As Robert Sokolowski argues, humans, unlike animals, are agents for truth. We are made to recognize and respond to something that exists out there and then to make declarations about that to others. Evolutionary accounts too quickly dismiss the complexity of this search for truth and the unique role that language plays in it.

So far I have addressed the limitations of metaphysical naturalism by turning to artists who have no cause for agreement with theological explanations for art. But in this chapter I want to illustrate what emerges when the artist is committed to the idea that aesthetic vision and theological vision work the same way. Flannery O'Connor built her entire oeuvre around the phenomenological and theological question of recognition. For her, both art and theology hinge on proper recognition and representation of the world as it is, and in particular, the true nature of human persons. O'Connor believed that recognition starts with the body, as it does for nonhuman animals. But she also believed that human consciousness has a uniquely native capacity for recognition of realities that exist but are not so easily discerned, like invisible ink, radio waves, or (far more tellingly) moral truths. Spiritual realities—like the inherent dignity of life or the primacy of love— cannot be recognized without this extra capacity. *Wise Blood* illustrates that aesthetic and theological understanding is a function of the whole person, and in the whole person wise blood is both "blood" and "wise." "Wise blood" is first an *instinctual, prelinguistic, and animal sense in the brain and the blood (the body)* of things, but it is also the *wise, linguistically structured experience* of things fundamentally exterior (or "real") that gets a rational treatment of some sort in the form of assent or rejection. Another way to put this is to say that O'Connor's novel is best understood phenomenologically, for it reveals that the purpose of language is the recognition of deeper realities, what Iris Murdoch called the "really real." This chapter is about what language, especially in the form of storytelling, is *for.*

WISE *BLOOD*: THE HUMAN ANIMAL

By any accounting, *Wise Blood* is a remarkable novel. It tells the story of Hazel "Haze" Motes, a lonely Southerner who believes in Jesus but tries to convince himself that he does not. He moves to a larger town "to do some things he has never done before." He starts the "Church Without Christ," preaching a "new jesus" that does not demand anything of anyone. "It's the church that the blood of Jesus don't foul with redemption," he declares.[6] But the hound of heaven chases him through the most unlikely of hosts: Enoch Emery. Enoch's wise blood leads him to bring Haze a shriveled corpse that he says is the new jesus Haze has been preaching. In a story that is all about what Haze wants to see, refuses to see, and actually sees, Haze recognizes that this corpse represents the true end for humans without Jesus, and he throws it against the wall in utter rejection. By this act he begins to return to the beliefs he thought he had left behind.

One of the strangest things about this novel is how full it is of animals and animal imagery used to describe humans. Most critics appropriately argue that O'Connor relies on this imagery to illustrate human degradation, but this is only part of the story.[7] O'Connor does it initially to establish that we have much more in common with the animals than we would sometimes prefer to admit.[8] *Wise Blood* has thus proven to be a prescient text. It depicts what twenty-first-century cognitive sciences are learning about all human cognition: it begins in the body.

This emphasis on the wise blood of the body is best seen in the character of Enoch Emery, the most animalistic of them all. The narrator observes at one point that he had "yellow hair and a fox-shaped face" (20) and at another that he "looked like a friendly hound dog with light mange" (23). Enoch lives by instincts and habitual behavior, a nearly entirely (merely) embodied existence.[9] He goes about his day in the exact same way: to work, to the Frosty Bottle, to the swimming pool, to the zoo, and repeat. So much is he a creature of habit that he makes Haze go with him through all these motions before he will take him to the Hawks' house. The narrator describes his behavior as instinctual, as a kind of knowledge in his blood. "Thinking" comes second to him, if it comes at all.

> Enoch Emery knew now that his life would never be the same again, because the thing that was going to happen to him had started to happen. He had always known that something was going to happen but he hadn't known what. If he had been much given to thought, he might have thought that now was the time for him to justify his daddy's blood, but he didn't think in broad sweeps like that, he thought what he would do next. Sometimes he didn't think, he only wondered; then before long he would find himself doing this or that, like a bird finds itself building a nest when it hasn't actually been planning to. (73)

Enoch behaves like the animals. But he also behaves like any human infant. In his book *The Body in the Mind*, Mark Johnson argues that the kind of meaning infants make of the world is "immanent, preconceptual, and non-propositional."[10] They respond in a very plastic way to their environment, which they perceive primarily through their bodily interactions with other humans. Johnson contends that this prelinguistic meaning is the foundation of all forms of meaning, not just our unconscious ones, and continues throughout our adult lives. Our knowledge is thus not inferential; it is "directly grasped." A metaphor commonly used for understanding—"he grasped my meaning"— is thus quite accurate. Enoch's wise blood works this way; it grasps at understanding his world.

Enoch Emery's animal nature might be the best evidence we have that O'Connor was not afraid of the fact that humans are primates with little genetic variation from other species. Because although Enoch behaves like an animal most of the time, only the fact that he is a *human*

animal can explain his later actions in the novel. As Johnson goes on
to argue, one of the earliest things that human infants do is separate
"human" from "other than human." Quoting Hillary Putnam, he reminds us that "our realism is 'realism with a human face.'"[11] True to
form, Enoch unconsciously longs for the genuine human connection
that the town of Taulkinham has denied him. O'Connor indicates this
repressed need by Enoch's reaction to the movie star who plays "Gonga"
the ape. While Enoch is on the way to deliver the new jesus to Haze,
he "found himself facing a life-size four-color picture of a gorilla" over
whose head was written "GONGA! Giant Jungle Monarch and a
Great Star! HERE IN PERSON!!!" (100). He interrupts his mission
to wait in line with children half his age in order to insult Gonga. But
when the time comes, he is so anxious about meeting him that he
"couldn't think even of the insulting phrases he used every day" (102).
So instead of insulting Gonga, he reaches out to try to connect with
him. The scene is quite sad. The actor took Enoch's hand with an "au-
tomatic motion," but "it was the first hand that had been extended to
Enoch since he had come to the city. It was warm and soft." The narrator continues, without irony:

> For a second he only stood there, clasping it. Then he began to
> stammer. "My name is Enoch Emery," he mumbled. "I attended
> the Rodemill Boys' Bible Academy. I work at the city zoo. I seen
> two of your pictures. I'm only eighteen year old but I already work
> for the city. My daddy made me com . . ." and his voice cracked.
>   The star leaned slightly forward and a change came in his eyes:
> an ugly pair of human ones moved closer and squinted at Enoch
> from behind the celluloid pair. "You go to hell," a surly voice in-
> side the ape-suit said, low but distinctly, and the hand was jerked
> away. (102)

O'Connor is obviously critiquing our "aping" of celebrities, and
revealing the extent to which human beings fail to act like human
beings. But in accord with G. K. Chesterton's idea that "the more we
really look at man as an animal, the less he will look like one," she emphasizes that even Enoch's behavior shows that to be human is to reach
beyond instincts to things that cannot be easily accounted for by them.
And those things require language.

Wise Blood: The Language Animal

In spite of years of scientific and nonscientific efforts to prove otherwise, the primary observable difference between animal and human cognition is the native capacity for flexible symbolic language, especially as revealed in the desire and ability to create linguistic art.[12] This is not to say that all animal species lack this capacity in the same way or to the same extent, or even that they always will. People have indeed trained individual members of a few different primate species (Kanzi the bonobo, for instance) to understand and employ a limited symbolic language. What this means (or doesn't mean) for the differences between humans and other primates is the subject of intense debate within and outside the scientific community, often driving people to absurd claims on either side. The confusion caused by these claims motivated the linguist Derek Bickerton, in his fascinating book *Adam's Tongue*, to clarify the issue with two points. First, even after the hours of intense human effort that are required to teach even limited symbolic language to animals, nonhuman primates do not speak or use signs in a way similar to human language, including American Sign Language. Second, nonhuman species that remain in the wild do not show signs of developing language.[13] In short, as far as we know now, *symbolic language use is not a native capacity of nonhuman animals.* But more to my purpose here, recent experiments by neuroscientists reveal that nonhuman primates have mirror neurons and will imitate others' actions, but they do not perform acts of mimesis. They do not create images to show to other primates as a means to communicate symbolically or connect emotionally.[14] Even when taught to use words, primates show no interest in basic aesthetic behavior. In short, as far as we know now, *artistic language use is not a native capacity of nonhuman animals.*[15] At the very least, these profound differences raise questions about why humans, and not other species, evolved these capacities. These questions remain unanswered.[16]

I am certainly not going to answer them here. But my thesis does not require me to. As I mentioned earlier, my primary concern in differentiating human behavior from animal behavior is to challenge the naturalist's "nothing but" conclusions that often motivate efforts to erase or trivialize these differences and what they might mean.[17] And

here is where Flannery O'Connor's *Wise Blood* is a particularly illuminating text. Enoch Emery may look and act like an animal in some
ways, but his instincts are wiser than those of any animal. He zeroes in
on something invisible to the naked eye: the meaning of the mummi-
fied corpse. Though Enoch does not fully understand what he is doing,
his effort to show it to Haze is a symbolic one that requires human language. Showing it to someone is an aesthetic act.

O'Connor emphasizes the aesthetic nature of Enoch's act by locat-
ing the corpse in the "Muvseevum" in a glass case. The first thing that
Enoch does when he meets Haze is to take Haze to see it. He claims
that he had been waiting for a sign to indicate who he should show it
to. "'You got to see it,'" Enoch tells him. "'When you see it, something's going to happen'" (52). When they get to the shriveled man,
O'Connor takes care to emphasize that Enoch means for Haze to recognize something in the corpse. "All he could tell was that Hazel
Motes's eyes were on the shrunken man. He was bent forward so that
his face was reflected on the glass top of the case. The reflection was
pale and the eyes were like two clean bullet holes" (56). The aesthetic
act brings Haze, too, at first to only unconscious cognition. He does
not yet understand that what he is seeing is a mimetic representation,
an image of his "new jesus," an image of his own destiny as a believer
in the Church Without Christ. He just knows he wants to get away as
fast as possible.

Enoch doesn't give up that easily. Since Haze refuses to acknowledge the corpse to his satisfaction, Enoch decides to steal it. Before
he brings it to Haze, he puts it in an elaborate washstand-turned-
minishrine in his own house. He sees the corpse as the literal thing that
Haze now worships in his Church Without Christ. This grotesque
substitution is at the heart of O'Connor's drama of recognition. Enoch
is not interested in the corpse for itself (purely animal instincts would,
of course, lead him away from such a thing). He wants to show it to
Haze. It is the mysterious meaning of it *for Haze* that draws Enoch to
it. As an aesthetic act it is analogous to O'Connor's sharing this grotesque story with us. And because it is, looking closely at it can help us
to answer the question, what is really going on in any aesthetic act?
What is really going on in the art of storytelling?

Again we must return to phenomenology and theology. In phenomenological terms, when Enoch brings the corpse to Haze, it is an

intentional, public action dependent on shared consciousness. Enoch's actions require more than the signal systems most animals use to communicate, and more than the protolanguage that some animals possess. It requires language.[18] Sokolowski explains that in phenomenology, the word *intentionality* means more than its conventional definition of being deliberative or purposive (as I was largely using the term in chapter 3). Intentionality is a doctrine that states that consciousness is never free floating; human beings have consciousness *of* something or someone that actually exists in the world. Without intentionality, our worlds would be incurably private; we would have no shared consciousness. Intentionality is thus descriptive of our search for meaning in the world, a search that is conducted linguistically. Indeed, the fact that we are language animals is what reveals this intentionality. Language is made possible by shared recognition of things that exist outside of our immediate consciousness of them. Thus, for Sokolowski, Charles Taylor, Hans-Georg Gadamer, and many others who work within this tradition, language is the thing that defines us as human, for it means that we are "truth seekers." Only language animals are oriented to the beyond. Indeed, as Taylor argues, "as human beings we live inescapably in a larger social, and even cosmic, context."[19] One might even conclude that we were designed to do so.[20]

To say that language animals are "truth seekers" is to say they recognize distinctions that are necessarily lost on protolinguistic animals. Important among these distinctions are those involving moral values. Taylor explains that only language animals can identify certain actions or ideas as worthy of desire or rejection, because these kinds of identifications "raise issues of intrinsic rightness."[21] When a person's intentionality "goes public" in any declarative statement, and even more, in a poetic one, it reveals the possibility of the accuracy or inaccuracy of that person's recognition of truth—especially truth that lies beyond the visibly factual. (An example of such a judgment would be, "Human beings should not be enslaved to other human beings.") Sokolowski, referencing Husserl, argues that language does not impose form on experience; instead "it emerges from and within experience as a formal structure of parts and wholes. It arises in the way things can be presented to us: they can become articulated, their wholes and parts shaken out and their formal structure made explicit."[22] In Heideggerian terms, an unconcealing of something in the world takes place, and in our recognition or our failure to recognize, we take a position for which we are responsible.

It is important enough to the argument I am trying to make in this book that language acts are understood to be the products of conscious, intentional interactions between a person and other things or persons, as Husserl insisted. But Sokolowski moves beyond Husserl's tendency to describe articulation and understanding as a matter of an individual's *private* consciousness. Sokolowski emphasizes that linguistic understanding is not the product of a solitary mind but is necessarily intersubjective. "When human beings disclose things, they do not act like impersonal drones or machines or solitary scouts," he explains. Language proves that we are embedded in relations with others. Language is not psychological as much as it is public.[23] The goal is shared recognition, and the responsibility that comes with it.

Since even the most basic linguistic predication is inherently intersubjective in its truth seeking, how much more is storytelling! But the really liberating thing about understanding the language animal as the truth-seeking animal is how it can bring us safely back to that much maligned theory of the arts as imitative. Back, in short, to mimesis. I do not have the space here to fully explain the rise and fall (and perhaps resurrection?) of this ancient theory, but a shorthand version can be seen in Gadamer's book *The Relevance of the Beautiful*. Gadamer argues that western philosophy has misread Plato's famous quarrel between the philosophers and the poets, which should be read ironically. Because of this misreading we have inherited a definition of mimesis as simple imitation: making a copy of an original. This, in turn, reduces the idea of recognition in a work of art to discerning how close the copy is to the original, which misses the point of art entirely. Gadamer notes that Aristotle's definition of mimesis was much richer. The mimetic arts work because they create a spark of recognition, often by way of deliberately unrepresentative things. The delight we take in the work of art is the delight of shared recognition, not the delight in seeing how "true to life" the work can be.[24]

For my purposes, it is illustrative to consider how Brian Boyd deals with mimesis. In a single paragraph, Boyd dispatches centuries of analysis of the idea of art as imitation. Assuming that mimesis is merely making a copy of an original, he argues that mimetic theories fail because they cannot easily explain most music or abstract visual art. What's more, they "do not explain why one species has evolved to develop a compulsive delight in fictional representations."[25] But when mimesis is recovered as an act of intersubjective communication intended to spark recognition, it easily explains all of these things—and much better. We make up stories because we were created to learn things about the world that only human beings can learn. We make up stories because they are the only way to see and to say the truth that lies beyond them. Homer depicted Sirens so that we could understand temptation. Shakespeare invested Prospero with magical powers so that we could think more deeply about art and the artist. Melville wrote "Benito Cereno" to implicate us in our racist reading of the world we think we see. Cormac McCarthy created Judge Holden so that we could recognize the Holdens in our midst. In every case the compulsive delight we have in fiction comes from the delight we have in recognition of a truth that just could not be seen if the seer had no soul. If the seer were not human.

Wise Blood is O'Connor's dramatization of this view of art. As I mentioned above, when Enoch steals the new jesus from the museum to show it to Haze, he is engaging in an aesthetic action. He recognizes that there is something about this shriveled mummy that Haze needs to see. The plot boils down to Haze's response: will he acknowledge the truth of this thing in the world, or will he go back to his necessarily privatized insistence that the world is the way that he wants it to be? Haze had been claiming, "I AM clean," and that his new jesus was superior because he has "no blood to waste." But Enoch recognizes, if unconsciously, that if you put your trust in materialism, this corpse is what you get. This is why O'Connor insisted that the meaning of the new jesus consists in its rejection.[26] In her estimation, Haze's recognition was made possible by Enoch's intentionality.

FROM PHENOMENOLOGY TO THEOLOGY

If this phenomenological account of recognition is correct—that consciousness must be consciousness of something real that can be recognized publicly, in shared language—then the door to theology must be reopened. It is simply irresponsible to exclude the possibility that art does not merely *make something special*, a view that nearly all evolutionary accounts share, but that it *recognizes when something actually is special* and thereby requires a response.[27] This is Flannery O'Connor's view of storytelling. Her goal was to see, to say, and to show the world the way she understood it to be in actuality: the creation of a personal God. O'Connor knew by instinct that the question of the proper recognition of reality is the question at the center of aesthetic vision *and* theological vision.

Understood in this way, O'Connor's view is very like that of Hans Urs von Balthasar, whose multivolume *Glory of the Lord* project was written, in part, to illustrate that theological vision is necessarily aesthetic. Drawing primarily on Aquinas, Balthasar argues that human beings, in order to see theological truths, must recognize the "whole form" of reality, and this whole form is necessarily larger than what an individual is able to discern without help. Human understanding begins with the senses but does not end there. Language capability and the corresponding aesthetic capability are given to human beings to ensure that they are open, "in knowledge and in love," to other people and ultimately to God. Balthasar writes that "it is *as a whole* (through all his faculties) that man is attuned to total reality."[28] In contemporary terms, nonconscious cognition and all embodied reactions come first and are necessary for accurate recognition. Balthasar writes that the "*cum-sentire*, 'to feel with,'" is prior to the "*assentire*, 'to assent to.'" Furthermore, "in the animal this occurs instinctively, but in man this accord is from the outset bound up with a certain spiritual delectation."[29] This is both an ontological and epistemological claim, and it can be traced definitively to Aquinas. Humans are able to see theological truths in Being itself by way of (and only by way of) the whole person. To see theological truths requires help, and for the same reason. From Aquinas, what we can know is limited by our mode of knowing. Our mode of knowing is experiential, participatory, embodied: wise blood.

I have argued from the beginning of this book that aesthetic vision is necessarily theological. At this point I am able to add that aesthetic vision is necessarily theological *because* theological vision is necessarily aesthetic. I am not trying to be cute, nor do I believe that my reasoning is circular. As I explained above, for Balthasar, theological vision does not start with rational assent to propositions but with an *experience* of being. We perceive the form with our senses before we understand it. In this insistence, Balthasar is merely building on the long tradition within Christian theology that exists in the church fathers, from Irenaeus to Augustine to Aquinas. The incarnation of Christ teaches us that experiential contact with the mystery of created being is the first step in perceiving the "really real."[30] Jens Zimmermann's excellent book *Incarnational Humanism* traces this idea from its origins to its persistence in sacramental traditions today. He argues that the church fathers insisted on a "participatory ontology" that defies the dualisms (mind/body, nature/grace) that continually threaten it.

That is how theological vision is necessarily aesthetic. Aesthetic vision is necessarily theological to the extent that God is real, we live in God's creation, and God entered space and time in a human form *in order that* we might see him. If this is indeed the case, to be true to the world as it is, is to be true to God, too, whether or not the artist wants to be. God's "invisible attributes, namely, his eternal power and divine nature, have been clearly perceived, ever since the creation of the world, in the things that have been made."[31] If God is real, to deny what we have perceived with our wise blood, as Hazel Motes clearly tries to, will not change this objective reality any more than claiming the earth is flat will cause it to become so.[32]

But we do deny what our wise blood shows us, and we deny it all the time. It is easier to stick to surface-level seeing that requires no answerability. Balthasar might as well have been describing Hazel Motes when he wrote that the apostate provides a kind of negative proof of God's existence because the apostate is one who has seen something and then denied it: "Through and through, he remains branded by the image he rejects: with terrible power this image leaves its imprint on his whole existence, which blazes brilliantly in the fire of denial."[33] Haze is branded in precisely this way. The harder he tries to dislodge what he has seen, the stronger it pulls him back. He cannot undo the shocking jolt of recognition he has experienced. He believes that Jesus is a fact, and his wise blood brought him back to that fact.

Flannery O'Connor was a cradle Catholic, so it is not surprising that she saw the incarnation as the ultimate reality and wrote fiction centered on its recognition. But O'Connor was not the only American novelist who understood that understanding starts in the body but ends in the soul. Nor is she the only novelist who saw brokenness as a reliable gateway to recognition of the whole persons we were created to be. Toni Morrison's greatest novel of spiritual recognition, *Beloved*, works this way as well. And that is where I turn next.

CHAPTER FIVE

Beyond the Postsecular

The Theological Grotesque in Toni Morrison's *Beloved*

This is what God does and this is who God is: the phil-
anthropos, the lover of the human being.

—John Behr

If we don't see that the choice is inevitable between the two
supreme models, God and the devil, then we have already
chosen the devil and his mimetic violence.

—René Girard

Since its first appearance in the late twentieth century, the concept of the postsecular has maintained a strong current in contemporary philosophy and literary studies. What scholars mean by the term can vary quite widely.[1] But within American literary studies, scholars tend to share a certain tone: they are circumspect and often openly suspicious when it comes to professed religious belief. Many of these studies feel as if they have come from scholars trained in the age of theory, an age that taught them, among other things, to subordinate personal faith commitments while privileging the cultural work texts do over any transcendent truths they might represent. Tracy Fessenden, for

A version of this chapter first appeared as "The Demonic in Service of the Divine: Toni Morrison's *Beloved*," *South Atlantic Review* 69, no. 3–4 (2004): 51–80.

example, simplifies American Protestantism in order to describe the tradition as an effort at cultural domination.[2] John McClure, albeit with the best intentions, sets up a rigid dichotomy between faith and religion, in which faith is good and religion is bad.[3] In this dichotomy, faith is free and expansive, and religion is necessarily authoritative and enclosing. To be postsecular, argues McClure, is to offer something that looks and feels like religion but without any proscriptions. It is characterized by a kind of thinking "that repeats the possibility of religion without religion."[4] In short, American writers employ a rather milquetoast "strategy of perhaps" and thereby rescue spirituality from the inherent violence of dogma.[5]

As the rest of McClure's study proves, for writers like Don De-Lillo, Thomas Pynchon, and Tony Kushner, this strategy makes sense. But has the systemic suspicion of organized religion and actual belief caused any critical blindness? Has it led to limited readings, or even to misreadings, of some of our contemporary novels? To answer that question I turn to a favorite novelist of postsecular theory, Toni Morrison. McClure walks an interesting line with Morrison since it is clear (even to McClure) that she does not see theistic faith and formal religion as mutually exclusive. Morrison "rejects fundamentalism, but she also refuses to reduce the traditional church to a vessel of oppression or to insist that the alternative spiritualities of people like Baby Suggs and Consolata are without their own risks and excesses."[6] But rather than revise his dichotomy, McClure concludes that in Morrison's text, faith in God is necessarily "partial" and does not rely on truth claims. Similarly, Amy Hungerford argues that Morrison flatly rejects the traditional authority of the Bible or organized religion in favor of its structure of internal allusiveness. She thereby "gathers all literary authority into herself" like Hungerford sees in Cormac McCarthy's work.[7]

I contend that with Morrison's work, especially a text like *Beloved*, this view is crippling. In its desire to reject religious misbehavior, it drains the power from a novel so defiantly insistent on spiritual realities. *Beloved* is unhesitant and unapologetic. It is more premodern than it is postmodern or postsecular. It illustrates that the literary artist's power is at its height not by borrowing authority from scripture but when she embraces one of the oldest and most universal of all plots contained therein: light has come into the darkness, and the darkness has not overcome it. *Beloved* is a grotesque novel, and the power of the grotesque depends on the world viewed theologically.

The Grotesque

"124 was spiteful. Full of baby's venom."[8] With these opening words of her most celebrated novel, Toni Morrison ensured that she would be remembered as one of the masters of the grotesque. The grotesque reveals by way of contradiction, and it is difficult to think of something more shocking and incongruous to us than a spiteful ghost of a murdered baby haunting its mother with such intensity. And this ghost eventually becomes even more shocking: it takes on flesh, grows up, and moves into the house. All of this is proof that Morrison knows her audience well. We like our hauntings to remain abstract, and therefore hardly know what to think when this spirit insists on being something more than a psychopathological fantasy, sitting down as it does with the other characters to eat breakfast.

But as shocking as this ghost is for contemporary readers, Morrison's literal use of the grotesque is quite conventional. The oldest appearances of the grotesque were the demons and gargoyles of painters and sculptors who actually believed in them—and in the corresponding angelic realm. These artists were trying to make the spiritual world visible to those who could not—or would not—see it. It is clear from Morrison's interviews that she grew up with a family who, like these artists, did not find appearances from the beyond merely a psychological projection of troubled souls. In short, they were believers. And instead of chastising them as one might expect from an enlightened scholar, she insisted that her family's experience of spiritual realities informed her sensibility as a writer.

> They had visitations and they did not find that fact shocking and they had some sweet, intimate connection with things that were not empirically verifiable. It not only made them for me the most interesting people in the world—it was an enormous resource for the solution of certain kinds of problems. Without that, I think I

would have been quite bereft because I would have been dependent on so-called scientific data to explain hopelessly unscientific things and also I would have relied on information that even subsequent objectivity has proved to be fraudulent, you see.[9]

Morrison's antimaterialism is not merely a novelistic device; for her, much of human experience is "hopelessly unscientific."[10] To rely on beings that appear from another realm is to insist, at the very least, that there are spiritual forces—forces for good and forces for evil. My argument thus begins with the observation that Beloved—whatever else she may stand for aside—is a demonic powerhouse.[11] This ghost is out to destroy Sethe and her family by crushing her spirit. And as soon as Morrison chooses to give real power and agency to the world of the beyond, she is also choosing to employ the grotesque in a conventionally theological way. The novel is thus powerfully premodern and rejects secular attempts to disenchant human experience.

Religious artists have often chosen to use gargoyles and devils to explain spiritual problems—particularly to warn us about encroaching evil, whether spiritual, physical, or moral. In his essay on the theological uses of the grotesque, Roger Hazelton argues that the "demonic is a matter of existential, and so of aesthetic, concern only for those who have faith in the divine."[12] And, he adds, it is a matter of aesthetic concern only for those who ultimately believe that the divine is good, more powerful, and ultimately in control of the demonic. With a phrase that is precise but a bit of a mouthful, Paul Tillich named such an appearance the "divine anti-divine ambiguity of the demonic."[13] In other words, God lets confusion reign by allowing the demonic to have its way for a time, only to completely thwart it in the end.

The devil isn't given his day only because it makes for a more interesting narrative. Instead, the purpose of the demonic grotesque is to demonstrate that the total revelation of evil—its full disclosure—is the necessary precursor to our struggle and victory against it.[14] The demon in *Beloved* makes a powerful appearance. Mimicking God, it demands total devotion, but behaving as a demon, it feeds like a parasite on being. But for all its power, it is clearly in the service of good, for, paradoxically, the more powerful the demonic becomes, the more it enables Sethe's ultimate healing. Indeed, Sethe is freed from a living death and psychological slavery precisely at the moment in which the demonic makes its ultimate demands. And in this story about love, it is when the demonic most insists that love be reduced to the strangling reality of possessive desire that it is forced to yield to the greater power of love as charity.

To insist that Morrison's use of the grotesque is theological is not at all to limit its rich symbolic significance, which has been aptly demonstrated.[15] Morrison resisted narrow readings of her novels, especially those that failed to take her fiction on its own terms and start with that. She tried to teach her students to "trust the tale and start with what you have."[16] If we take that advice and also take a step back from the fiction as a whole, we find that the tale that Morrison tells over and over again is, at one level, remarkably simple. Her stories are about love and its absence, and they operate with the oldest narrative motivations: catharsis and revelation in characters and readers.

I am not making a claim here that Morrison's ideas are explicitly or solely Christian; Morrison, following generations of African Americans, clearly draws religious ideas both from Africa and from the West. But far from the watered down versions of Christianity mentioned by McClure, she insists and demonstrates that African Americans found in authentic Christianity something that they needed to survive: a distinct focus on love. Not the western definition of erotic love, which Morrison saw as narcissistic and destructive, but love as charity extended through community to the "least of these." Morrison said that it was these "love things" that were "psychically very important" to a people who have had to live a life of struggle against rage.[17] Africans coming to America incorporated Christianity into their spiritual lives because it included "the openness of being saved" and insisted on a transcendent love available to the "lamb, the victim, the vulnerable one who does die but nevertheless lives" (117). In other words, what appealed to them—in spite of the slaveholders' abuse of Christianity— was the core of the gospel, the oldest promise of redemption and acceptance. "You were constantly being redeemed and reborn, and you couldn't fall too far, and couldn't ever fall completely and be totally thrown out.... Everybody was ready to accept you" (117).

It is with this same "openness of being saved" that Toni Morrison begins *Beloved*. As Margaret Atwood argues, the epigraph from Romans 9—"I will call them my people, which were not my people; and her beloved, which was not beloved"—speaks to inclusiveness.[18] It is the promise of acceptance for a people previously scorned and rejected. It is, in short, a promise that good will win out over evil, no matter how powerful the evil. Morrison insisted that she wanted to dust off old myths like she dusts off words, and here she uncovers and represents the oldest of Christian myths: the devil will have his day, but love will prevail in the end.

THE GRIP OF THE DEMONIC: DESPAIR

When the novel opens we find the demonic in control because Sethe is immobilized in despair. Isolated and scapegoated by the rest of the community, Sethe is perishing in stasis. By not actively choosing life, or trying to create a different future, she defaults to death. Indeed, to Sethe, "the future was a matter of keeping the past at bay. The 'better life' she believed she and Denver were living was simply not that other one" (42). She is thus a model for Kierkegaard's definition of the "sickness unto death." For Kierkegaard, despair is a spiritual problem; it describes the condition of people who are not rightly related to themselves, who do not really have a self. It is important to point out that Sethe's murder of her baby daughter only activated a deeper despair that had been there all along. Kierkegaard gives an example of a woman who has lost her lover; the loss merely reveals the self she never had: "This self of hers, which if it had become 'his' beloved, she would have been rid of, or lost, in the most blissful manner—this self, since it is destined to be a self without 'him', is now an embarrassment; this self, which should have been her *richesse*—though in another sense just as much in despair—has become, now that 'he' is dead, a loathsome void, or a despicable reminder of her betrayal."[19] Sethe, had her daughter lived, would have still been living in despair (thinking of her children as her only good thing) but would have been a step further removed from ever discovering it.

The consciousness that one is in despair is the beginning of the way out of it, but no such recognition has been available to Sethe for eighteen long years. Her best hope for spiritual healing—receiving Baby Suggs's lessons on loving one's own self—was lost when Baby Suggs gave in to her own despair, a situation that the narrator points out in the opening pages: "Suspended between the nastiness of life and the meanness of the dead, she couldn't get interested in leaving life or living it, let alone the fright of two creeping-off boys" (3–4). This suspension is the condition that Kierkegaard describes as the living death of despair: "despair is the sickness unto death, this tormenting contradiction, this sickness in the self; eternally to die, to die and yet not to die, to die death itself."[20]

To keep people in a living death is the oldest goal of the demonic.[21] And this ghost is remarkably successful with that task until Paul D shows up. Paul D's appearance is an immediate threat to the ghost because he represents the possibility of Sethe's healing from despair—her hope for movement, growth, change—in short, new life. This potential new life for Sethe begins where it must, by Paul D's simple expressions of love and care for Sethe that make her believe that she might be able to muster the courage to begin the pain of remembering (both her victimization and her own violent acts) that will finally begin her healing process. In the tender acceptance of his embrace, she wonders if "maybe this one time she could stop dead in the middle of a cooking meal—not even leave the stove—and feel the hurt her back ought to. Trust things and remember things because the last of the Sweet Home men was there to catch her if she sank?" (18). The ghost pitches the house in protest. This is going to be a battle.

Initially Paul D wins that battle, and overcomes the ghost's power by coaxing Sethe and Denver out of the seductive trap of 124 and into the community's participation in a carnival. As Susan Corey points out, Morrison's use of the carnival here clearly suggests the positive grotesque as illuminated by Bakhtin.[22] Carnival represents everything that Sethe does not have: activity, fun, community, change, and new possibilities. Carnival celebrates a common humanity; it is the place where we laugh at ourselves, especially at our embodied existence. In this way, carnival epitomizes the positive grotesque, exaggerating the fact that our bodies are always changing, growing, transforming. Thus, as Bakhtin emphasizes, the laughter of carnival is productive; emphasizing sexuality and birth, it is "always conceiving."[23] This carnival spirit enters Paul D, Sethe, and Denver. Paul D can come into their lives as a productive father, with new energy and growth—a possibility at first only adumbrated by the shadows of the three walking together.

Their shadows are holding hands behind them on the way there, then leading them on the way back, suggesting that this new future is now within reach. "Nobody noticed but Sethe and she stopped looking after she decided that it was a good sign. A life. Could be" (47).

Since real life is the only thing that can loosen the grip of a living death, the ghost must now act more aggressively to keep its control. By the time the three get home from the carnival, it has emerged from the water, a fully grown woman now, and meets them at the house. The event is powerfully grotesque in its affront to readers' expectations. When we witness Sethe's sudden urge to urinate in a way that suggests her water is breaking, we know that Beloved is meant to represent the lost baby. But what is not immediately apparent to Sethe or to readers is whether this being is there to do good or evil. But readers quickly find out the answer to that question when Beloved begins to act in conventionally demonic ways. As René Girard explains, the devil can only be a parasite on being, one that functions by seducing its victims into making their own bad choices.[24] And right from the start, this ghost's mode is seduction. It does not break in; it gets itself invited in. It gets itself fed and nurtured by promising love and attention. Its seductive power becomes most apparent in the way it has its way with Paul D, breaking up the potentially life-giving relationship between him and Sethe and moving him slowly out of the house, room by room.

But as powerful as this demonic ghost is, its power is markedly less than that of the divine because it cannot give or produce. It can only take away or destroy. Its power is like that of a vampire: it sustains itself on the lifeblood of others. The shared characteristic of all demonic grotesques is that they cannot act authentically but can act only by way of imitation. Beloved fits Girard's definition of Satan in that its methods are necessarily mimetic. "Satan does not 'create' by his own means," Girard writes. "Rather he sustains himself as a parasite on what God creates by imitating God in a manner that is jealous, grotesque, perverse, and as contrary as possible to the upright and obedient imitation of Jesus. To repeat, Satan is an imitator in the rivalistic sense of the word. His kingdom is a caricature of the kingdom of God. Satan is the ape of God."[25] Beloved clearly apes the Christian God in order to rival God and to keep Sethe from healing. The demon becomes flesh, promises a biblical and pure love reminiscent of that from the

Song of Songs, and seduces Sethe and Denver to form a perverse trinity with it. But because this anti-divine is ultimately in service to the divine, the demonic plan backfires.

APING GOD: INCARNATION

It is easy to see why some critics have argued that Beloved functions as a kind of Christ figure in the novel. She is spirit become flesh, and her incarnation does, after all, ultimately lead to Sethe's healing. But I think that it is more accurate to argue that Morrison offers Beloved as the ape of God, as a demonic being that tries the same strategies but desires completely opposite ends. There are two aspects of the incarnation of Christ that Beloved's incarnation controverts to try to keep Sethe from healing: the acceptance of the body and the acknowledgment of the reality of time in human redemption.

First, when God chooses to become man in the incarnation of Christ, the action itself validates the beauty of creation, indicating that all human flesh has value. In short, it is God's primary way of calling his people Beloved—in soul *and* in body. The theology of the incarnation has thus been the Christian church's answer to the western tendency toward Gnosticism—separating the soul from the body and valuing only the soul. *Beloved* implicitly argues that slavery as an institution is anti-Christian and essentially Gnostic because the body is seen only for what it can do or accomplish—not for having value in and of itself, simply because the person is made by God. When Baby Suggs preaches in the Clearing, she is preaching against the degradation of slavery by insisting on the spiritual value of the body. She insists that because the community cannot rely on others putting value on their flesh for itself, they must learn to do so themselves: "No, they don't love your mouth. *You* got to love it. This is flesh I'm talking about here. Flesh that needs to be loved. Feet that need to rest and to dance; backs that need support; shoulders that need arms, strong arms I'm telling you. And O my people, out yonder, hear me, they do not love your neck unnoosed and straight. So love your neck; put a hand on it, grace it, stroke it and hold it up" (88). In the theology of the incarnation, it is human flesh as well as spirit that has value and should be loved and cherished. Emily Griesinger thus turns to Baby Suggs's sermon in order to reply to critics who argue that Morrison's work is more pagan than Christian. "Not *typically* Christian in its emphasis on the holiness of the flesh, Baby Suggs' sermon is *genuinely* Christian nevertheless in understanding that salvation includes the body and in recognizing that God does not look on outward appearance but penetrates the heart."[26]

Second, Christian theology teaches that God, an eternal being, had to cross incongruously (and grotesquely) into time in order to redeem humanity. Jesus's literal suffering, death, and resurrection are essential to the insistence that salvation for the Christian is never symbolic. In other words, the Christian conception of time is linear, not cyclical. Human redemption requires the passing of time; it requires that the redeemed one's past action can remain in the past, and not be held against her. But Beloved, as a demonic force, is a vampiric, undead being whose goal is the exact opposite of God's. Her task is to convince Sethe that time is cyclical and that she can never be truly free from the pain of her past except in death. She is trying to convince her to reject her own embodied existence completely in order to become free. Since this is the lie that Sethe already believed (proven when she killed her baby daughter in order to set her free), it is one that the demon has little difficulty seducing her with again.

This two-part demonic seduction can be seen in the section in which Beloved's voice is made identical to those of the victims of the middle passage. All of these bodies are dead now, but their souls seem to live on, on the other side, existing in a place that sounds a lot like a conventional description of the eternal torments of hell. "All of it is now it is always now there will never be a time when I am not crouching and watching others who are crouching too I am always crouching the man on my face is dead" (210). Beloved's goal is to seduce Sethe to achieve "the join" with her, which sounds like sexual union that will efface all individual identity.

> I follow her we are in the diamonds which are her earrings now my face is coming I have to have it I am looking for the join I am loving my face so much my dark face is close to me I want to join she whispers to me she whispers I reach for her chewing and swallowing she touches me she knows I want to join she chews and swal-

lows me I am gone now I am her face my own face has left me I see me swim away a hot thing. (213)

Sethe's beloved daughter is dead, we must never forget. For Beloved to act in this world she has to drain life from someone else. Thus the "join" of Sethe with this Beloved can ultimately only be the join of death, not of life. And Sethe, living in utter despair, is ready and willing to go down to this death. She thinks that she is taking Baby Suggs's advice to "lay it all down, sword and shield" and live, but really she is moving toward death, as she tells Beloved:

> When I put that headstone up I wanted to lay in there with you, put your head on my shoulder and keep you warm, and I would have if Buglar and Howard and Denver didn't need me, because my mind was homeless then. I couldn't lay down with you then. No matter how much I wanted to. I couldn't lay down nowhere in peace, back then. Now I can. I can sleep like the drowned, have mercy. She come back to me, my daughter, and she is mine. (204)

The "peace" that she can have now can only come at the cost of choosing not to live, not to struggle. Beloved's ultimate aim is to get Sethe to go all the way with her despair—to lock herself in the house and starve to death.

But as powerful as the demon's seduction is, it is in this aping of the incarnation that the demonic sows the seeds of its own destruction and ends up serving the divine—and all because of the logic of the grotesque. The incarnation of Christ is grotesque because its shocking connection of human and divine is necessarily revelatory. In the incarnation, ultimate good appears in human form, healing and blessing. It reveals love. It shows the way and does it; it does not just teach about it. Likewise, Beloved's very appearing ensures that eventually she will be seen for what she is: a wolf in sheep's clothing.

And most important, it is in its grotesque insistence on incarnation that Beloved as ghost most parallels *Beloved* as text. When an interviewer told Morrison that her books had a haunting quality, Morrison was delighted. She wants her fiction to demand active participation from readers, like the call and response of black preaching. "I want a very strong visceral and emotional response as well as a very clear intellectual response," she explained.[27] The logic of the grotesque in fiction, in other words, is inherently incarnational precisely because it insists that one's intellect cannot be separated from one's bodily experience. As Geoffrey Galt Harpham argues, the grotesque appeals to the parts of us that know instinctively that we cannot just vault over real pain and suffering by an act of will. The grotesque heals "the self divorced from the raw material of life and provid[es] a tonic affirmation of the wholeness of existence. . . . [I]t is one of the large paradoxes of wholeness that it cannot be imagined or figured except as a violation of natural laws, in monstrous or distorted form."[28]

Morrison turns to the grotesque because she wants her readers to enter the pain of Sethe's past experiences as much as she wants Sethe to do so. It is a shock to anyone's efforts to deny the impact of America's slaveholding past as much as it is to Sethe's denial of her own past. But the shock is also what makes experience thoroughly redemptive. For although the grotesque brings the real pain of Sethe's past and the "60 million and more" victims of slavery to life, it also thereby proves that these past sins will ultimately fail to destroy Sethe and the African American community. Through the demonic grotesque, the past makes the redemptive "mistake" of drawing attention to itself, revealing the evil, injustice, and suffering for all to see. Theologically considered, the grotesque teaches us that evil can be more easily rejected when it is more clearly seen. When it appears so boldly, the community will no longer be able to ignore it; this is the truth to which Ella attests when she explains why she went on to participate in the exorcism at 124: "Whatever Sethe had done, Ella didn't like the idea of past errors taking possession of the present. Sethe's crime was staggering and her pride outstripped even that; but she could not countenance the possibility of sin moving on in the house, unleashed and sassy" (256). When the demon is forced to be sassy instead of seductive, we know its time is nearly up.

APING GOD: EROTIC LOVE

According to the logic of the grotesque, for Sethe's redemption to be complete, the devil must have its day first. Beloved is—and must be—

nearly successful in her mission to keep Sethe in a living death before this final exorcism can take place. Therefore, to try to achieve her goal, the ghost apes God not only in its incarnation, but in her fundamental offer: love. But the love the demonic offers is a corrupt love that thrives on absence instead of presence. In other words, she can only offer love as possessive desire (worship of the god Eros), not love as charity. This is the distinction that Trudier Harris develops in her essay "Beloved: Woman, Thy Name Is Demon." Harris argues that the driving force behind the story is Beloved's insatiable desire—not real love, which requires an act of the will. Desire, argues Harris, is "unbridled id, self-centered and not to be easily denied," but will can be altruistic—it can want the other's best. Beloved, continues Harris, "is the personification of desire [and] thus epitomizes the demonic. . . . [S]he is the objective, physical distillation of desire."[29]

To take Harris's argument a step further, the demonic not only personifies desire, but she tries to seduce Sethe and Denver into substituting insatiable desire that can only end in death for a healthy love that can give life. She does this by distortion, by calling desire love and demanding total allegiance thereto.[30] I believe that Morrison's tour de force in *Beloved* is her ability to suggest that the western world has been seduced by this particular demonic lie for a long time—and is spreading the contagion mercilessly. A world that can countenance the possession of human beings as chattel will know no end to the thinking that others exist to serve me or to fill a lack in me. When love is reduced to desire, the other, the beloved, is seen only in terms of possession and ownership, not as being-in-itself with value for itself. It is not too much of a stretch to suggest that it is something that Sethe learned from the culture of the white slaveholding South that leads her to believe that she had only two choices to make when schoolteacher showed up at 124: her children would be owned by schoolteacher or owned by her. And since she had no legal right to motherhood at this point, her choice was to draw them to herself into the ultimate "safety" of death, where nothing could be dirtied. It is an outcome forced by a slaveholding society: seeing no inherent value in herself, Sethe needs to possess her children at all costs. "The best thing she was, was her children. Whites might dirty *her* all right, but not her best thing, her beautiful, magical best thing—the part of her that was clean" (251).

One of the most vital contributions that Girard has made to our understanding of how evil operates in society is to articulate a concept that he calls "mimetic contagion." Girard argues that it is mimetic desire—the desire to possess what others desire—that defines us as human beings and is the source of all violent conflict.[31] The notion of imitative desire becomes even more complex when illustrated in the context of slavery. The African American community in *Beloved* has been doubly contaminated in that they had never been permitted to have their own desires or had much of an opportunity to see themselves as something other than property. The long denial of the legitimacy of an entire community's desires has contributed to the degradation of love and sexuality to mere possession, trade, and ownership. When we first meet Sethe, we discover that she has traded ten minutes of sex in order to get the engraving "Beloved" on the tombstone of her dead daughter. In addition, the first sexual encounter between Paul D and Sethe is marked by the classic devaluation of the other that takes place when the beloved has been treated as a fantasy to be possessed and not an equal to be loved—the goal of a long unrequited desire. Desire always promises the fantasy but cannot help with commitment. After their desire is consummated, "Paul D saw the float of her breasts and disliked it, the spread-away, flat roundness of them that he could definitely live without, never mind that downstairs he had held them as though they were the most expensive part of himself" (21). Because Sethe and Denver have for eighteen years been turned inward, unhealthily dependent on and possessive of each other, it is no wonder that the incarnated ghost easily seduces Denver, who immediately loves Beloved with a "breakneck possessiveness" (54).

That Morrison wants to link this perversion of love (as possessive desire) to the logic of slavery is nowhere more evident than in the scene in which Sethe returns to the Clearing. Overwhelmed by the flood of memories in Paul D's return, as well as by the pain of "new pictures and old rememories" (95) such as her discovery of her husband's mental breakdown, Sethe returns to a place she associates with redemption and healing. In this place Baby Suggs, holy, taught the people how to claim ownership of themselves, to love themselves because no one else would. Sethe reflected on the twenty-eight days she had to learn that lesson from the community as "days of healing, ease and real-talk. . . . Bit by bit, at 124 and in the Clearing, along with the others, she had claimed herself. Freeing yourself was one thing; claiming ownership of that freed self was another" (95). In the Clearing now, eighteen years later, Sethe longs for the feel of Baby Suggs's caressing fingers on her neck because she longs for affirmation and love. What she feels first as caressing fingers become strangling ones as the ghost Beloved apes a healthy love by loving too much, demanding too much—in short, needing too much. It is love trapped in an infantile state. "They stayed that way for awhile because neither Denver nor Sethe knew how not to: how to stop and not love the look or feel of the lips that kept on kissing. Then Sethe, grabbing Beloved's hair and blinking rapidly, separated herself. She later believed that it was because the girl's breath was exactly like new milk that she said to her, stern and frowning, 'You too old for that'" (97–98). Later Beloved denies that it was her doing the choking: "I kissed her neck. I didn't choke it. The circle of iron choked it" (101).

In Morrison's telling, the circle of iron and the strangling hands of too thick love are, at the root, the same trouble. Love that imitates slavery is no love at all. But the lies of the devil have to be partial truths in order to be effective. They must always *feel* good and *seem* to be right. The demonic agent here apes God by seeming to satisfy Sethe's deep desire to love her dead daughter and to be loved and forgiven in return. After all, this ghost has a justified claim: she (and the 60 million and more victims) *should have* been loved and allowed to live. But turning to absence to fill an absence shows the very core of Sethe's problem. Loving others as a way to fill a void, to meet the need of an empty self, always ends in the excesses of possession and, ultimately, in destruction. This is what Baby Suggs was beginning to learn about "whitepeople" that was infecting their community by way of mimetic contagion. In the days before the "misery" (Sethe's murder of her daughter) and at the height of Baby Suggs's ministry to others, 124 had been a "cheerful, buzzing house where Baby Suggs, holy, loved, cautioned, fed, chastised and soothed" (87). She could do this ministry only because she had learned before the others did that her heart was her own, not the possession of someone else, and that no one can love anyone from a deficit. This is why in those days, "talk was low and to the point—for Baby Suggs, holy, didn't approve of extra. 'Everything depends on knowing how much,' she said, and 'Good is knowing when to stop'" (87). But her daughter-in-law's action breaks even Baby

Suggs's huge heart, and she gives up, announcing to Sethe and Denver "the lesson she had learned from her sixty years a slave and ten years free: that there was no bad luck in the world but whitepeople. 'They don't know when to stop,' she said" (104).

No one who is insufficient in themselves, and thereby infected by the logic of possession and desire, will ever know when to stop. The excess of the party that Baby Suggs held the day before "the misery" began is an example of how the contagion was spreading. The feast started out with a couple of buckets of Stamp Paid's blackberries and then grew. There was nothing wrong, of course, with the idea of feasting, but there is an implication of real pride in Baby Suggs's offerings. With pride and envy corrupting the feast, the community began to feel less complete in and of itself and began to covet, to desire what belongs to others. "Too much, they thought. Where does she get it all, Baby Suggs, holy?" (137). And they begin to think that Baby Suggs is taking over God's rightful position: "Loaves and fishes were His powers—they did not belong to an ex-slave who had probably never carried one hundred pounds to the scale, or picked okra with a baby on her back" (137). At this point contagion is imminent. Baby Suggs herself begins to wonder if she has crossed the line, and it is right at this moment that she can smell evil coming. The "dark thing" coming is the four horsemen, the fugitive slave catchers, whose grabbing at Sethe's children cause her to make the ultimate act of possession.

It is no surprise that when the murdered baby returns it operates entirely under this logic of love as possession and seduces others accordingly. It is covetous, greedy, possessive—Eros gone bad because it has been given too much power. Morrison was clearly thinking about western culture's worship of Eros when she began to compose this novel. In 1983 she told Claudia Tate that "love, in the western notion, is full of possession, distortion, and corruption. It's a slaughter without the blood."[32] The ghost participates in a bloodless slaughter in its attempts to completely consume Sethe. Some of Morrison's most powerful passages illustrate this aggressive possessiveness.

> Rainwater held on to pine needles for dear life and Beloved could not take her eyes off Sethe. Stooping to shake the damper, or snapping sticks for kindlin, Sethe was licked, tasted, eaten by Beloved's eyes. Like a familiar, she hovered, never leaving the room Sethe was

in unless required and told to. She rose early in the dark to be there, waiting, in the kitchen when Sethe came down to make fast bread before she left for work. In lamplight, and over the flames of the cooking stove, their two shadows clashed and crossed on the ceiling like black swords. She was in the window at two when Sethe returned, or the doorway; then the porch, its steps, the path, the road, till finally, surrendering to the habit, Beloved began inching down Bluestone Road further and further each day to meet Sethe and walk her back to 124. It was as though every afternoon she doubted anew the older woman's return. (57)

In this passage Morrison emphasizes how Beloved's eyes consume Sethe. As Jean-Pierre Vernant argues, the erotic experience, in its need to possess the other, privileges sight. The longing of those under the spell of Eros is fundamentally narcissistic, a longing to see one's self reflected in the beloved's eyes. He writes, "Each of the two partners acts as a mirror for the other, as he perceives his own reflection in the other's eye, and pursues it with his desire."[33] This is exactly the sort of relationship that Beloved pulls both Sethe and Denver into in order to efface their distinctiveness entirely. Speaking about Sethe, Beloved insists, "I am not separate from her there is no place where I stop her face is my own and I want to be there in the place where her face is and to be looking at it too a hot thing" (210).

By erotic seduction, the ghost pulls both Sethe and Denver with her into an isolated circle. To illustrate the power of erotic desire, Morrison draws on language from the biblical book Song of Solomon—a move she has made before.[34] This text has long been treated by Christian exegetes as a metaphor for Christ's love for the church, a love that encompasses a healthy longing because it will end in an appropriate consummation in due time: Christ will return and receive the Beloved. In *Beloved* Morrison seems to be more interested in defying any interpretation of the Song of Songs that sees it as putting a biblical stamp of approval on possessive desire between human lovers. Love that is too thick—or as the Song of Songs puts it, "as strong as death"—is not a good thing. It is demonic to offer love that feels good but also makes demands that can never be satisfied. The sweets of the biblical Song of Songs in this text become symbolic of Beloved's insatiable appetite for only the sweet, infantile aspects of love—not the demanding, adult parts. Living inside of possessive desire tastes good but cannot ulti-mately be nourishing. At 124, there is only the sweetness of seduction that leads ultimately to a starved isolation and death. This narrow eroticism can never widen into a love feast to which all are invited and at which all flourish.

APING GOD: AN UNHOLY TRINITY

Beloved's most aggressive and perverse imitation of God is her effort to pull Denver and Sethe with her into an atemporal trinity. The nar-ration of the "unspoken" voices of this unholy trinity comprises the book's poetic core.[35] Morrison presents Sethe's first-person narration, then Denver's, then Beloved's, and then brilliantly braids them into what she calls a "threnody" of voices, characterized by an otherworldly intimacy that does not require language. Morrison explains that "the section in which the women finally go home and close up and begin to fulfil their desires begins with each one's thoughts in her language, and then moves into a kind of threnody in which they exchange thoughts like a dialogue, or a three-way conversation, but unspoken—I mean, unuttered. Yet the intimacy of those three women—illusory though it may be—is such they they would not have to *say* it."[36] Each of the three sections illustrates the desire of the speaker to possess the beloved other. Sethe begins: "Beloved, she my daughter. She mine . . . I won't never let her go" (200). By the fourth section the individual voices have melded together in a kind of narcissistic identity.

> Beloved
> You are my sister
> You are my daughter
> You are my face; you are me
> I have found you again; you have come back to me
> You are my Beloved
> You are mine
> You are mine
> You are mine.
>
>   (216)

The emphasis on three is evident here: three voices, nine lines, the triple repetition of desire for possession. What is less evident is that by inviting them into a self-sufficient, "loving" trinity, Beloved has seduced them with a version of the devil's oldest temptation—that they could become like God. Beloved promises them the eternal self-sufficiency, and love in identity, that is the province only of the holy Trinity. Denver and Sethe are not immortal beings. They cannot, without dying, step out of time, language, and the problem of otherness—in other words, the risks of human life, the potential of others to hurt you. There is no such safety in life because no one can love perfectly except God.

It is in Morrison's grotesque perversion of the holy Trinity that her reliance on an essentially Christian definition of love becomes most evident. The traditional Christian explanation of the Trinity—the distinct but united beings of the Father, Son, and Holy Spirit—is that it exists because love requires a relationship among persons in order to be clearly seen. God, who is love, becomes visible in the act of loving the Son.[37] Following this kind of thinking, Saint Augustine describes the various persons of the holy Trinity as lover, beloved, and love itself. The Trinity illustrates charity because its very existence as three emphasizes the need for an other to be loved (the beloved) in order that love itself become visible. Augustine also argues by extension that any time you see charity, you see a trinity: "For when we love charity, we love her loving something."[38] Though Augustine's argumentation is often very abstract, he makes it clear that this Trinity he describes is anything but abstract. Indeed, the holy Trinity only operates because the Father and the Son are each in and of themselves full and complete beings who are secondarily in relationship with each other. The language with which Augustine makes the point particularly pricks our ears in this context.

> What it comes to is this: every being that is called something by way of relationship is also something besides the relationship; thus a master is also a man, and a slave is a man, and a draught-animal is a horse, and a security is a sum of money. Man and horse and sum of money are said with reference to self, and signify substances or beings; while master and slave and draught-animal and

security are said with reference to something else, to signify certain relationships. But if it were not, for example, a man, that is some substance, there would be nothing there that could be called master by way of relationship . . . so if the Father is not also something with reference to himself, there is absolutely nothing there to be talked of with reference to something else.[39]

Augustine's primary point is that being must come before relationship for that relationship to have meaning. And Morrison would find unwitting irony in this passage, because the master-slave relationship has been thoroughly deconstructed in our age: we now take it as axiomatic that "master" has meaning only because of the primacy of his relationship to his slave, whose very existence defines him. It is because there is no essential being in the master that he needs his slave to define him and sustain him. A lack of self leads necessarily to perversion of relationship.

But in *Beloved* Morrison does not go the whole way with some contemporary thinkers and insist that there is no self to be had. To believe that is, for Morrison, to give in to the logic of slavery. The slave system contaminates everyone but especially newly freed blacks who had no opportunity to learn how to fully own themselves. Without proper self-ownership, people can only love too little (to hold on too loosely) or too much (to fully possess). When the demon Beloved apes God, she cannot offer true charity, which depends on being; she can only offer a perverse version of love. She can only offer lack, desire, need, and covetousness. Thus the healthy lover, beloved, and *love* itself modeled in the holy Trinity is replaced at 124 Bluestone Road by two needy beloveds and *desire* itself. It is no wonder that both Sethe and Denver begin to literally melt away in the presence of this vicious, insatiable vampire. When Denver thinks of herself without Beloved, she panics: "If she stumbles, she is not aware of it because she does not know where her body stops, which part of her is an arm, a foot or a knee. She feels like an ice cake torn from the solid surface of the stream, floating on darkness, thick and crashing against the edges of things around it. Breakable, meltable and cold . . . she can feel her thickness thinning, dissolving into nothing" (122–23). Denver knows she is losing herself: "This is worse than when Paul D came to 124 and she cried helplessly into the stove. This is worse. Then it was for herself. Now she is crying because she has no self" (123). Denver panics having to deal with another leaving, and she "doesn't move to open the door because there is no world out there" (123).

The demon wins if she convinces mother and daughter that there is no world out there and no individual selves of value in here. For a time she succeeds. The false feeling of love and safety is so strong that Sethe now consciously reinterprets the previous hope she had had for a new family with Paul D as an ill-fated hope for this new narcissistic trinity: "Obviously the hand-holding shadows she had seen on the road were not Paul D, Denver and herself, but 'us three'" (182). Sethe now believes that the world is in this room. She has been thoroughly deceived by a Platonic erotic vision of unity, where bodies (which are only carriers of pain after all) can be left behind in the merging of the soul with the eternal. This whole is realized "not by joining the two halves of the body, and superimposing the navels, but by tearing the soul from the body, reintegrating the part into the Whole, making the center of the individual coincide with the universal center, fusing the self with God."[40]

But the eternal join promised by the demonic is an illusion. There can be no holy Trinity of created, temporally bound, human beings, and there can be no genuine love between people who do not fully own and love themselves. Sethe begins to have her life completely sucked from her, and she ultimately and willingly exchanges places with Beloved by becoming the infant herself: "The bigger Beloved got, the smaller Sethe became. . . . [S]he sat in the chair licking her lips like a chastised child while Beloved ate up her life, took it, swelled up with it, grew taller on it" (250). But it is at this point—the full revelation of the grotesque—when the demonic aping of the holy Trinity necessarily breaks down. Charity, which is the basis of the holy Trinity, welcomes others, delights in new beloveds. It is dialogic. But possessive love, built as it is out of need, is necessarily jealous. It is univocal, and ends in the silence of death in identity.[41] A trio of erotic lovers will never work, and Denver soon recognizes that she is the third wheel in this relationship. With the little bit of outside perspective the jilting gives her, she is finally able to see that they were "locked in a love that wore everybody out" (243). The situation has become desperate. She knows they need help, and she goes out to find it. When she leaves the house it is April, the season of Easter. Their redemption is about to begin.

REDEMPTION BY REVELATION

Denver's move out into the community parallels the earlier move when the three had gone to the carnival. But there is a difference now. Denver finds that, in order to explain how badly she needs help, she must repeat some of the trio's "unspeakable thoughts unspoken" to the neighbors. In particular, she must tell the story in order to get entrance to the Bodwins—the white family to which she turned for employment. Janey, the housekeeper, will not let her see them until Denver answers her questions about what is wrong with Sethe. So Denver considers the situation and decides to reveal the truth. "Nobody was going to help her unless she told it—told all of it" (253).

The fact that the "unspeakable" story is now being told and retold in the black community and beyond is the proof that the demon's plan has completely backfired. Her incarnation into intelligible visibility was the beginning of her demise.[42] She had hoped to lure Sethe and Denver into the silent circle of iron, in which living being is totally enslaved to an unspoken, fragmented story, a narrative that only gets told internally, repeated compulsively, but never escaped from precisely because it remains untellable—unfinished. A cycle, not really a narrative. With the fragments of her life in that state of formlessness its hold over Sethe *would* be eternal. But to organize the story, to step into language, to force the appearing of Beloved and *Beloved*, is a redemptive act of incarnation. All the suffering is there for everyone to see. To tell the story as a complete narrative is to step out of the illusion of timelessness and step back into the normal passage of time. It is to insist that the story of Sethe's pain had a beginning and can have, finally, an end. *Beloved* as text gathered all of the pieces of Sethe's story into her own growing body, and she would have remained powerful only if she could have remained invisible, and the story she represents, forgotten.[43] But the work of the incarnation and the grotesque that follows its logic is always revelatory, and Denver leaks the story. She bears witness. She speaks the ghost that she has seen into words. Beloved becomes a story, and in the telling, her end is near.

And this is largely because the healthy telling requires a response. It requires a community. The end result of Beloved's appearance and her attempt to control Sethe's life completely is that the community can no longer conscionably ignore Sethe's pain and continue to ostracize her. Their collective exorcism is more than a move to help Sethe out of her despair; it is a way, the only way, for them to end the mimetic contagion that had led them to make Sethe their scapegoat. It is to now turn their energies, instead, against evil itself.

By reading the ghost Beloved as a demonic agent that needs to be exorcised, we can also see where Morrison locates divine activity in the world. There is never a deus ex machina in Morrison's work; God manifests himself in an accepting, loving, and charitable community. The communal exorcism defies the western conception of the heroic ascendancy of the individual and returns to what John D. Zizioulas argues has always been the teaching of the Christian patristics about the Trinity and the church; namely, that the "substance of God, 'God,' has no ontological content, no true being, apart from communion."[44] Zizioulas is not arguing for pantheism but rather insisting that the holy Trinity is a person, not a substance, and that love makes God what he is. It is not at all a stretch to argue that in their undeniably loving exorcism, the community of black women functions like a church. The voices of the women "searched for the right combination, the key, the code, the sound that broke the back of words. Building voice upon voice until they found it, and when they did it was a wave of sound wide enough to sound deep water and knock the pods off chestnut trees. It broke over Sethe and she trembled like the baptized in its wash" (261). In Beloved, Morrison's triumph is to show that evil, when perpetuated by a community motivated by fear, is best defeated by a community motivated by the baptizing power of love. But she also lets the demonic show its grotesque face just long enough to prove that it was in the service of the divine all along.

CHAPTER SIX

Beyond Beauty

Theology on *The Road*

Where's the road to the place where light dwells;
    darkness, where's it located?
Can you take it to its territory;
    do you know the paths to its house?
    —Job 38:19–20 (Common English Bible)

Every act for the sake of the good is a subversion of the logic of materialism.

—David Bentley Hart

The Road is a novel that seems to dwell entirely in darkness. It begins after some planet-level devastation has long ago reduced the world to ash. The protagonists, a man and his son, are in a struggle for their lives. They encounter cannibalism, slavery, cold-blooded acts of violence. Cormac McCarthy's narrative is as stark and cold as his plot; this is fiction that cuts to the bone. Engaged so elementally with matters of

---

This chapter uses material taken from *The Image of God in an Image Driven Age*, edited by Jeffrey W. Barbeau and Beth Felker Jones. Copyright 2016. Used by permission of InterVarsity Press, P.O. Box 1400, Downers Grove, IL 60515, USA; www.ivpress.com.

life and death, *The Road* makes a case for itself as a classically natural-istic novel. The environment thwarts the characters. Chance dictates almost every encounter. Characters beg for God with no expectation that he will show up.

The bleakness of this novel, keeping step as it does with other recent American novels, is in part what prompted Paul Elie to argue that fiction has "lost its faith." For a country where millions of people profess faith in Jesus Christ, he argues, our literary fiction is strikingly and incongruently post-Christian. In our fiction, Christian belief figures "somewhere between a dead language and a hangover." There's language that echoes the transcendent but has no confidence in it. McCarthy and Don DeLillo feel like prophets, "but Christianity in their work is a country for old men."

Elie is not alone. Amy Hungerford, in her book *Postmodern Belief*, reads McCarthy's *Blood Meridian* as a prime example of a larger trend in American fiction of drawing on biblical language as a way of giving a book the feeling of scripture's moral authority when the book's actual authority is merely aesthetic. "We are left," says Hungerford, "with the presumptuous creation of a prose that sounds like scripture, tempts one to read (for metaphysical structures) as if one were reading scripture, and yet withholds all but the aesthetic and sentimental effects of scripture. In this sense, McCarthy has written, in *Blood Meridian*, a sentimental novel of the highest order."[1] *The Road* fares no better. Through its beautiful language, McCarthy transforms "Biblical authority into literary authority reconceived as supernatural authorship or rhetorical power."[2]

No matter how one reads our so-called postsecular moment, Hungerford's argument about contemporary American literature is powerful and difficult to refute. Allen Ginsberg wanted his openly irreligious poetry to be chanted like a mantra. DeLillo's novels self-consciously offer fully immanent, rhetorical substitutes for religious transcendence even while many of his characters seem to suspect that such substitutes are not enough. But I argue that Cormac McCarthy's interaction with the Bible and its role in American religious consciousness is of an entirely different order from that of either Ginsberg or DeLillo. Though McCarthy himself professes no belief, engagement with metaphysics and theology is foundational to his fiction. To borrow Flannery O'Connor's description of the South, his landscapes are "Christ-haunted."[3] Intentionally or not, his narratives push against what Charles Taylor calls a "closed immanent frame": the modern conviction that humanity must bring its own meaning to an otherwise meaningless world.[4]

I make my argument in two parts. First, I show that, far from the Bible being a borrowed and merely aesthetic authority for McCarthy, his work evokes it in a way that forces the astute reader to return to it. In *The Road*, the book of Job and all its metaphysical questions regarding personhood and suffering is placed in the foreground. Second, this novel's beauty is not best explained by an effort on McCarthy's part to replace God's authority with beautiful prose. Instead, like the book of Job itself, the novel must be beautiful to the extent that it is answerable to the goodness of human persons as made in the image of God. *The Road* exists under what Hans Urs von Balthasar has called the "demand of the beautiful," and it pulls its readers—however unwittingly—to respond to that demand.

ECHOES OF JOB

Hungerford's argument that McCarthy's texts borrow the authority of the Bible without engaging its content relies on her positioning him in a long line of writers who conceive of the writer as playing God in assigning fates. But in the case of *The Road*, to compare the author (or the narrator) to God is a confusion. McCarthy himself is better likened to the storyteller of the book of Job, and the narrator of *The Road*, particularly when he is taking on the man's perspective, is less like God than he is like Job himself. The novel's situation and subsequent soul-searching thus evoke the biblical book most known for asking why the world is full of suffering and evil.

The book of Job is initially narrated like any conventional story. It begins, "There was a man in the land of Uz whose name was Job, and that man was blameless and upright, one who feared God and turned away from evil" (Job 1:1). Outside of the prologue and epilogue, the narrator of Job (similar to McCarthy in *The Road*) does not intervene to tell us how to interpret the story. The rest of the book of Job is composed, almost completely, of dialogue between Job and his counselors, and later between Job and God. While *The Road* is also written in the third person, it features a stronger and more active narrator who is separate from McCarthy (all of the time, since this is a work of fiction) and from the man (some of the time). The narrator of *The Road* sometimes renders judgment on the man and boy's situation, judgment that appears to be largely separate from the characters' point of view. That this is the case is undeniable at the end of the novel, where narration continues after the man's death. In spite of this separation, it is more frequently the case that the narrator delivers the man's perspective through free indirect discourse and similar means.

This matters because I contend that when the narrator's perspective aligns closely with the man's perspective, it mirrors Job's point of view and echoes the biblical language. We are being asked to compare their situations and their attitudes and to see their words in the mode of lament. Recall that Job has no idea why his world has suddenly fallen apart. He receives messengers, one after the other, who inform him that his livestock, servants, and entire family have been struck down and destroyed. He rips his clothes, shaves his head, and drops to his knees in despair. He has boils on his skin. He declares that he loathes his life (Job 7:16). He says he speaks with bitterness in his soul (Job 10:1). Although he does not curse God with his lips or charge him with wrongdoing, he laments his birth with intensity and poetic beauty.

> Let the day perish in which I was born,
>> and the night that said,
>> 'A man-child is conceived.'
> Let that day be darkness!
>> May God above not seek it,
>> or light shine on it.
> Let gloom and deep darkness claim it.
>> Let clouds settle upon it;
>> let the blackness of the day terrify it.
> That night—let thick darkness seize it!
>> let it not rejoice among the days of the year;
>> let it not come into the number of the months.
> Yes, let that night be barren;
>> let no joyful cry be heard in it.

Let those curse it who curse the Sea,
  those who are skilled to rouse up Leviathan.
Let the stars of its dawn be dark;
  let it hope for light, but have none;
  may it not see the eyelids of the morning—
because it did not shut the doors of my mother's womb,
  and hide trouble from my eyes.

                                        (Job 3:3–10)

The emphasis on darkness reveals the metaphysical weight of the passage. George Steiner argues that Job's lament of his own birth echoes
Jeremiah 20:14–18, but "in *Job* it is no individual, it is the cosmos which
is cursed. The day is to be made darkness, 'Let the stars of the twilight
thereof be dark,' let light go out undoing, un-creating God's primordial *fiat*."[5] When Job asks why he was born, comparing himself to the
"infant that never sees the light," he is not lamenting his individual
situation as much as declaring the "suffocating blackness" of extinction,
the anxiety over why anyone should be born only to face suffering
and death.
    The man's situation in *The Road* is as dire—and as weirdly severe—
as Job's. His lament also takes on cosmic proportions. At 1:17 on the
day his wife would give birth to his only son, the clocks stop and the
world as they had known it comes to an end, leaving them in a barren
landscape that grows increasingly cold and dark. Ash is everywhere.
There is a blackness that is so impenetrable the narrator insists it would
"hurt your ears with listening."[6] They walk in a "cold autistic dark"
where the only voices with any human feeling are their own. The narrator's tone, especially when clearly aligned with the man's, is as metaphysical as Job's: "On this road there are no godspoke men. They are
gone and I am left and they have taken with them the world. Query:
How does the never to be differ from what never was?" (32). Another
passage, ambiguous as to whether it is the narrator's or the man's perspective, reads, "Perhaps in the world's destruction it would be possible
at last to see how it was made. Oceans, mountains. The ponderous
counterspectacle of things ceasing to be. The sweeping waste, hydrop-
tic and coldly secular. The silence" (274). The man and his son have
long been abandoned by the suicide of their wife and mother, a woman

whose only answer, like that of Job's wife, had been to curse God and die. Their isolation is near-total. To read their story is to follow a small, flickering flame moving slowly in a field of utter darkness.

The silence surrounding the man and the boy as we follow their story is of pivotal importance. Are we to read it as the silence of God? If so, then the narrative's parallel with the book of Job is even more striking. For although the main part of Job consists entirely of dialogue, it is the dialogue of the false counselors who are trying to tell Job that his situation is his fault. Eliphaz is Job's first false counselor, and he talks a lot. He tries to tell Job that he is blessed because God has disciplined him. He counsels Job to trust that God is taking care of him, to know that all of this is for his own good. But Job is not persuaded. After Eliphaz stops talking, Job continues his own speech for two chapters more, saying, among other things, "For the arrows of the Almighty are in me; my spirit drinks their poison; the terrors of God are arrayed against me" (Job 6:4). When he addresses God, he questions him, very much like the man does in *The Road*: "Why have you made me your target? Why have I become a burden to you?" (Job 7:20).

In a scenario without sense, the false counselors try to explain God's actions. Job maintains his innocence throughout his lament, and the tension builds. Will God ever show up? Indeed, the best explanation for the fact that the book of Job is composed as a dialogue is because its primary issue is whether an absent God will appear and put Job's questions to rest. Job's cries and complaints "are best viewed as calls on the seemingly absent God to become present," and Job longs to be in a relationship "in which God would call and Job would answer (14:15)."[7] Job wants to hear from God, but he wants speech with the full authority of God's presence, not the rationalizing of the counselors. This helps us understand his famous monologue.

> Oh that my words were written!
> Oh that they were inscribed in a book!
> Oh that with an iron pen and lead
> they were engraved in the rock forever!
> For I know that my Redeemer lives,
> and at the last he will stand upon the earth.
> And after my skin has been thus destroyed,

yet in my flesh I shall see God,
whom I shall see for myself,
and my eyes shall behold, and not another.
My heart faints within me!

                    (19:23–27)

Job's desire to have his life recorded in a book corresponds with his de-
sire to see God, to know that God is there and is not silent. In short,
Job wants to know that God sees him. Job's "friends" can never explain
God's actions, and their presence cannot take God's place.

The dialogue scenario is evoked and inverted in *The Road*, but
the silence serves the same end. It centers on the same question: We
are here; we are suffering; where is God in all of this? When the man
addresses God, he also shakes his fist and pleads with God to show
himself.

> He descended into a gryke in the stone and there he crouched
> coughing and he coughed for a long time. Then he just knelt in the
> ashes. He raised his face to the paling day. Are you there? he whis-
> pered. Will I see you at the last? Have you a neck by which to
> throttle you? Have you a heart? Damn you eternally have you a
> soul? Oh God, he whispered. Oh God. (11–12)

The man's thoughts here are very different in tone from those of the
four men in the naturalistic story "The Open Boat" by Stephen Crane.
In that story, the men are in peril, and once it occurs to each that the
universe has no regard for him, "he at first wishes to throw bricks at
the temple, and he hates deeply the fact that there are no bricks and no
temples."[8] In *The Road*, the man audibly asks God if he exists and then,
like Job, shakes his fist at him in anger.

The longest conversation in the book is between the man and an
old man they meet on the road who calls himself Ely. Like Job's Eliphaz, he talks a lot, but his message is more like that of Job's wife—to
curse God and die. Although he says that words are useless, he uses
a lot of them: "I think in times like these the less said the better. If
something had happened and we were survivors and we met on the
road then we'd have something to talk about. But we're not. So we

dont" (171–72). But he does keep talking, telling them that he has known for a long time that there are no gods, and that it will be better when all the people are gone as well because "we'll all breathe easier." The man replies with a sarcastic edge, "That's good to know." Ely returns earnestly, "Yes it is. When we're all gone at last then there'll be nobody here but death and his days will be numbered too. He'll be out in the road there with nothing to do and nobody to do it to. He'll say: Where did everybody go? And that's how it will be. What's wrong with that?" (173).

These evocations of Job's situation make it impossible to side with James Wood when he argues that McCarthy's text is only theological at the end, not throughout.[9] Instead, the best explanation of McCarthy's choice to put the man and the boy in a stripped-down, postapocalyptic scenario is to exaggerate the greatest metaphysical and theological questions that face us all. We are all confronted with the brutal facts of our imperfect existence. We are all confronted with the fact that things fall apart. We are all confronted with the fact that we have the power to kill others and to destroy the earth. Why are things this way? Both Job and the man in *The Road* see themselves as cursed by God. But it is also true that the main thing they have in common is that neither one of them chooses to curse God in return, either by behaving like an animal or by taking his own life.

The Demand of the Beautiful

If I am correct that McCarthy is evoking the book of Job in order to draw readers into a metaphysical dialogue with it and not, as Hungerford would have it, in order to draw an ersatz authority from it, then there are several implications. The first, as I have already suggested, is that metaphysical questions regarding suffering, violence, and evil are engaged. But it also means that the question of whether God will show up in the end is more than just a matter of flipping a coin. It is a question written into the structure of the narrative itself, a point I develop later.

A second implication, perhaps not as readily apparent, involves the beauty of the language of the novel. Job is one of the most poetic books of the Bible, and most scholars would agree that its beauty serves a greater purpose than mere ornament. But beauty has a contested status: does beauty reside in the thing itself, or is it merely a matter of subjective taste? Is it universal, or is it a culturally constructed, fungible category? Although I do not have the space in this book to engage the beauty question thoroughly, my argument depends on an understanding of beauty that contains both objective and subjective aspects. I believe that when a narrative contains beautiful language, the most likely (but not necessary) explanation is that at least part of what we recognize as beautiful reflects an intersection with what we recognize as goodness and truth—categories that necessarily have theological resonances. I believe that the beauty of *The Road* is of this type.

I will make my case here, and in the following chapter, in conversation with Balthasar's theological aesthetics. In the first volume of *The Glory of the Lord*, Balthasar argues that beauty should not be considered apart from the other two (non-Platonic) transcendentals, truth and goodness.[10] For Balthasar, art for art's sake is thus a meaningless and destructive concept. When humanity no longer believes in truth and goodness, we sever beauty from them and make it into a mere mask, a surface thing with no capabilities greater than giving a few sensuous delights. "We no longer dare to believe in beauty and we make of it a mere appearance in order the more easily to dispose of it."[11] Since beauty is an inherent part of the truth and goodness of the world God has created, disposing of it in this manner is a human effort to reject the mystery of being. In so doing, we reject the creator of that mystery.

To make matters worse, when beauty is treated as mere appearance, the good of creation and in creation begins to lose its attractiveness to humanity. "Man stands before the good and asks himself why *it* must be done and not rather its alternative, evil."[12] Being gets translated into a mere "lump of existence," and humanity is no longer able to read its language, which is beauty. Beauty, when it is severed from goodness and truth, points only to itself and not to another being. Balthasar calls this aestheticism.

For Balthasar, it is possible to separate beauty from goodness and truth. When we make beauty into a mask that we can manipulate to our own interests, we go against our best God-given instincts. Primary among these instincts is the desire to go outside of ourselves in order to connect with an other, including the ultimate other, God. Art mirrors the choice to be in the world and act in the world as a choice made in freedom, a choice that has the additional effect of deepening self-understanding, deepening the self as a person in communication with others.[13] At this point Balthasar writes:

> Through his body, man is in the world. As he expresses himself, he acts and intervenes responsibly in the general situation. *He inscribes his deeds indelibly upon the book of history, which, whether he likes it or not, henceforth bears his imprint permanently.* Here, at the very latest, man must realize that he is not lord over himself. Neither does he rule his own being in freedom so as to confer form upon himself, nor is he free in his communication. *As body, man is a being whose condition it is always to be communicated;* indeed, he regains himself only on account of having been communicated. For this reason, man as a whole is not an archetype of Being and of Spirit, rather their image; he is not the primal word, but a response; he is not a speaker, *but an expression governed by the laws of beauty, laws which man cannot impose on himself.* As a totality of spirit and body, man must make himself into God's mirror and seek to attain to that *transcendence and radiance that must be found in the world's substance if it is indeed God's image and likeness—his word and gesture, action and drama.*[14]

Thus human being in its origin (being created in the image of God) is already "form"—a picture, an image, in some way, of God—and it cannot cease to be so.

My point is that McCarthy's prose is not beautiful because he wants his art to take the place of scripture. Instead, it is beautiful because it is Christ-haunted. Balthasar's passage best explains how that beauty operates. Note that the man's actions in the world of the novel do indeed make marks upon it: some good, some bad. And McCarthy, of course, is the one who records all of these actions in a book. As Job had lamented, "Oh that my deeds were written down," McCarthy attends to the man and the son by telling their tale in a dignified way that values their experience and calls it beautiful. As a storyteller he is a witness, and as readers so are we.

McCarthy has explored this view of storytelling as witness else-where, most notably in the novel *The Crossing*. In it, a lapsed priest tells the protagonist the story of an embittered old man he once ministered to. The old man had been through a Job-like experience, catastrophically losing his entire family while he was away. In deep grief, he went on a mad rant against God. What the priest claims he learned from this man boils down to the fact that the story itself is the most important thing. When that story is told to another—and now retold to the protagonist of *The Crossing* and to us—it reveals its value. Storytelling, however unwittingly, provides a witness to that value. It is a complicated interchange, but it ends with the priest affirming not the goodness of God (the priest had behaved toward the old man the way Job's counselors behaved toward him, trying to convince him of God's goodness) but the fact of God. God sees everything without needing to be seen. Nothing escapes God's aesthetic vision. Here the priest, referring to himself in the third person, concludes:

> What the priest saw at last was that the lesson of a life can never be its own. Only the witness has power to take its measure. It is lived for the other only. The priest therefore saw what the anchorite could not. That God needs no witness. Neither to Himself nor against. The truth is rather that if there were no God then there could be no witness for there could be no identity to the world but only each man's opinion of it. . . . Bear closely with me now. There is another who will hear what you never spoke. Stones themselves are made of air. What they have power to crush never lived. In the end we shall all of us be only what we have made of God. For nothing is real save his grace.[15]

Although we cannot be sure that McCarthy's opinion matches that of the priest, McCarthy's storytelling performs this grace-granting witness. As I have been arguing throughout this book, the storyteller's loving attention echoes the ultimate Other's witness to a world of human activity that would otherwise be meaningless. Indeed, God's existence as ultimate witness (Bakhtin's superaddressee) enables every other act of witness, for "if there were no God then there could be no witness for there could be no identity to the world but only each man's opinion of it."

Again, I am not trying to argue that storytelling proves the existence of God, or that McCarthy himself believes in God. Instead I am arguing that novels like *The Road*, whether considered postsecular or not, tacitly assent to Balthasar's argument that a human being cannot "confer form upon himself."[16] Even though he never names the man or the boy in *The Road*, McCarthy has set us up to see this particular man's and his son's lives as significant. McCarthy has drawn us to the beauty of this man's life and his struggle—and to the importance of his moral choices, his witness to the readers who will "hear what you never spoke."

In the next part of his argument, Balthasar insists that a person is not free in communication. A person is instead a being "whose condition it always is to be communicated," and the self is regained by this communication. The man and his story are communicated here; thus they participate in a kind of being, a fictional being that nonetheless relates analogically to the larger idea that all persons' lives are communicated to someone, somewhere, all the time. We are seen by God, and have been so from the beginning. By writing the story of this man and this boy, McCarthy participates in this idea—indeed, witnesses to it—intentionally or not.

In *The Road*, there are several places of open assent to this idea. In the first two pages of the book, we are introduced to the man, who awakens from a bad dream and reaches out for the boy to make sure he is there. From the first, this novel is about human connection. Before the boy wakes up, the man surveys the area, and we read that he "sat there holding the binoculars and watching the ashen daylight congeal over the land. He knew only that the child was his warrant. He said: If he is not the word of God God never spoke" (5). The man, who speaks very little throughout the novel, says these words aloud. McCarthy emphasizes this with the words "he said," which are often excised from the trimmed-down dialogue of the book. Thus the man literally communicates with the boy while also indicating that the boy is a communication of God. The man is not drawing a parallel between the boy and Jesus as the word of God, but the boy as a word spoken by God into existence. Aesthetic vision is, in this case, like divine speech-act theory; it requires one person looking at another, speaking the other into existence or acknowledging the other by speech.[17] The boy turns and opens his eyes, and we read the first dialogue:

Hi, Papa, he said.
I'm right here.
I know.
(5)

The fact that we are spoken into existence, as the word of God in creation, is for Balthasar the reason humankind is not an archetype of Being and Spirit, as if competing with God. We are instead made in the image of God. Humankind "is not a primal word," he argues, "but a response; he is not a speaker, but an expression governed by the laws of beauty, laws which man cannot impose on himself."

It is because of this that Jens Zimmermann argues, along with Balthasar, that theology "establishes aesthetics as integral to self-knowledge." Zimmermann provides his own translation of Balthasar: "All our acts of self-expression are embedded in history and leave traces we cannot alter. We are 'not original in being and spirit but copy, not original word but answering word, not freely speaking but expressed meaning, and therefore completely under the demand of the beautiful which we ourselves cannot control.'"[18] Following Balthasar, Zimmermann argues that recognition of the beautiful in the mystery of being has the inherent power to draw viewers into contemplation of something deeper. Humanity, made in the image of God, is beautiful and shows the beauty of all being. Jacques Maritain similarly argues that when something is beautiful, as such it "belongs to the kingdom of the spirit and plunges deep into the transcendence and the infinity of being."[19]

When aesthetics are properly bound up with the true and the good centered on the mystery of being, it is no longer possible to dismiss the ugliness of the postapocalyptic world McCarthy presents as theologically irrelevant or as hostile to theism. Nor is it possible to argue that McCarthy's theological passages are just tacked on in an attempt to make a materialistic and naturalistic novel appear metaphysical. Instead, the entire novel reveals that when humankind walks away from

God and turns the world into an ash heap, we make it harder, but not impossible, to recognize the beauty and goodness of creation. This partly explains why the novel is concerned so parabolically, archetypally, metaphysically, and theologically with darkness and light. The man and the boy face a world growing increasingly dim, indeed, the apocalyptic blight, whatever it was, is described as a "cold glaucoma dimming away the world" (3) and leaving them bereft of warmth and direction.

Seen this way, the expression "carrying the fire" has core significance. The man made up this expression to encourage the boy. It stands for, among other things, the fact that the man and the boy are trying to be the "good guys"—to not give up, to not eat people, to not kill anyone except when their immediate lives are in danger. In short, "carrying the fire" is retaining their humanity. In these actions they become a beacon of light in utter blackness, evocative of John 1:5: "the light shines in darkness but the darkness has not overcome it." Indeed, every time the man looks at the boy, he sees him as beautiful light, one so beautiful he cannot bring himself to take the boy's life in order to prevent others from hurting him.

> There were times when he sat watching the boy sleep that he would begin to sob uncontrollably but it wasnt about death. He wasnt sure what it was about but he thought it was about beauty or about goodness. Things that he'd no longer any way to think about at all. (129–30)

Of course, the man *is* thinking about beauty and goodness as he watches his child sleep, though the passage emphasizes that the structures that make these thoughts possible are quickly dissipating.[20] This is due in large part to the man and boy's increasing isolation in this world. But the structures for these thoughts exist for us as readers, and they are in this novel, which touches beauty and goodness in multiple ways and invites us to do the same.

To put it simply, this is not an ugly novel. It appreciates and depends on our recognition of the difference between light and dark, between goodness and evil.[21] Furthermore, the drama of the novel, like the book of Job, surrounds the question of whether the man will curse

God and die precisely because he and his son are losing any way of thinking about beauty or goodness—anything, in other words, that makes life worth living. This loss, not death, is what the man is sobbing about, and it is a powerfully theological moment.

Finally, Balthasar's insight that the human being is a communicated word helps us to understand the significance of the isolation the man and the boy experience in *The Road*. Though able to live on their own for quite some time, the novel begins with them being forced out of their isolation and onto the road. The man is rightly suspicious of most people they meet—people who have turned to evil ways to survive, who have abandoned loving cooperation for slavery and cannibalism. By the time we are introduced to the father and son, they have already become "each the other's world entire" (6), which is not, of course, a sustainable long-term situation. The boy instinctively knows this and is always trying to find others.

The power and logic of a plot forcing a man out of isolation to save his family becomes clear when we consider ongoing theological reflection on the doctrine of the *imago Dei*. Following the lead of Karl Barth, many theologians insist that loving dialogical relationships with others is the place where the image of God is primarily seen. For example, Alistair McFadyen writes, "Humanity is fully in the image of God only where it is a lived dialogical encounter."[22] Emmanuel Mounier makes a similar point, noting that the person as a created being exists only in relation to others, and this is especially revealed in communication.[23] Whether or not the image of God depends on personal relationship, the man and boy's isolation is a problem because it increasingly removes them from seeing the created goodness of others. They have each become the other's only means of seeing the image of God in the human world. This explains why the man and the boy are so desperate to continue speaking to one another, though their dialogue becomes quite clipped and dangerously self-imitative because of their isolation.

That isolation in *The Road* also helps to explain why the narrator and the man lament that language itself is dissolving along with the general de-creation of the world. As they camped,

he [the man] tried to think of something to say but he could not. He'd had this feeling before, beyond the numbness and the dull despair. The world shrinking down about a raw core of parsible entities. The names of things slowly following those things into oblivion. Colors. The names of birds. Things to eat. Finally the names of things one believed to be true. More fragile than he would have thought. How much was gone already? The sacred idiom shorn of its referents and so of its reality. Drawing down like something trying to preserve heat. In time to wink out forever. (88–89)

The worry is that the world of things is shrinking, and with it, the names of those things. Because the world is de-creating all around the man and the boy, eventually language itself is going to disappear, leaving a gray world with no distinctions whatsoever.

So how are we to read beautiful language in a book that is simultaneously describing the decay of things and of language? We have three options. First, as Hungerford might argue, the novel's beautiful language could be an effort to shore up against these ruins, with the artist taking God's place in creating the world through language. Second, the novel itself and its beautiful language could be simply a nostalgic remembering of a former beauty that is disintegrating. Or, third, the beautiful language could be insisting that as long as there are persons carrying the fire of goodness and truth, beauty is never really lost.

While I do not believe the first thesis for reasons I have described, the second remains compelling. The narrator provides numerous descriptions of the dissolving world that suggest in time the "sacred idiom" will "wink out forever." But if we read these laments over the dissolving world in light of their echo of the book of Job, the second thesis is harder to sustain. And the clearest bit of evidence against this thesis is the novel's ending: the discovery of the boy, after his father's death, by what appears to be a trustworthy community—with children. The father's sacrifice and refusal to curse God and die has not been in vain. As if that fact were not enough, McCarthy provides this penultimate paragraph:

The woman when she saw him put her arms around him and held him. Oh, she said, I am so glad to see you. She would talk to him sometimes about God. He tried to talk to God but the best thing was to talk to his father and he did talk to him and he didnt forget.

The woman said that was all right. She said that the breath of God was his breath yet though it pass from man to man through all of time. (286)

Against the silent waste of suicide and abdication, and specifically in the name of God, the boy talks to and does not forget his father. Of course there is nothing necessarily Christian about this particular conception of God, and it is not my purpose to argue as such. But it is certainly possible to read this passage as an example of God showing up in the primary way he does today: in people who name him as God and who love others in that name. This idea is consistent with Balthasar's insistence that the human is an image of God and a response, not an archetype and a primal speaker. Simply put, the passage is overtly theological in a way that McCarthy could have easily avoided. Consider the similarity of this passage to a quotation from Theophilus of Antioch:

God has given to the earth the breath which feeds it. It is his breath that gives life to all things. And if he were to withhold his breath, everything would be annihilated. His breath vibrates in yours, in your voice. It is the breath of God that you breathe—and you are unaware of it.[24]

God answers Job's queries not with explanations but with himself—his voice, his breath. Here, God answers the man's queries through this family that continues to talk about God and to God. What the boy finds in the end is not luck. It is goodness in the form of other persons who are also "carrying the fire." Luck is as impersonal as the flip of the coin; goodness, in our world, requires a human face. With this passage McCarthy reveals, intentionally or not, his great love for the father and the son, love that is too deep to either leave them in despair or to leave their story untold. He is their witness to us, and "if there were no God then there could be no witness for there could be no identity to the world but only each man's opinion of it."

If McCarthy's landscape is as Christ-haunted as I have argued that it is, we are left with the third explanation for the beauty of the novel. If the good, the beautiful, and the true are the imprint of God in the world, then these things will reveal him. If human persons are made in the image of God and are under the "demand of the beautiful," in the way that Balthasar describes, if persons are beautiful according to laws of being that they neither make nor control, then McCarthy is participating in this logic by making the language of *The Road* sing and hum. This is why, in his book on beauty, Roger Scruton argues that beauty cannot be considered a property that can be ascribed to some things to the exclusion of others. Beauty is more like a posture toward the things seen. A judgment for beauty "demands an act of attention. And it may be expressed in many different ways. Less important than the final verdict is the attempt to show what is right, fitting, worthwhile, attractive, or expressive in the object: in other words, to identify the aspect of the thing that claims our attention."[25]

This leads us to consider the immense, lamenting beauty of the last paragraph of the novel, clearly now from the narrator's point of view.

> Once there were brook trout in the streams in the mountains. You could see them standing in the amber current where the white edges of their fins wimpled softly in the flow. They smelled of moss in your hand. Polished and muscular and torsional. On their backs were vermiculate patterns that were maps of the world in its becoming. Maps and mazes. Of a thing which could not be put back. Not be made right again. In the deep glens where they lived all things were older than man and they hummed of mystery. (286–87)

Hungerford argues that "it is the words," not the carrying of the fire, "that hold out hope—that put the speckled trout back into the river and the river back into the valley and make things right again even as the words say these things cannot be done."[26] She reads the passage as McCarthy reveling in his God-like power. But to believe this requires readers to forget that, before this passage appears, we have spent 250 pages attentively following a man who loves his son and refuses to give in to evil. We have cheered on the father and son as they carry the fire, believing against their circumstances, as Job did, that a light still shines in the world and the darkness has not overcome it. What has greater power than a well-told story to draw our attention to the essential beauty of being that humanity is always and everywhere in danger of ignoring or desecrating? For we, like Job and like the man, have the choice of life or death before us all the time. If we choose to let it, the light of goodness and love in the world can indeed flicker and grow dim. Maybe McCarthy is more of a prophet of the end times than he knows. When the Son of Man returns, bringing justice, will he find faith on the earth? (Luke 18:8).

Perhaps McCarthy's final paragraph, emerging after the appearance of God in the loving faces and voices of the good family, prophetically warns us of our peril. It warns us that when we destroy our world or blur it beyond recognition, we lose. What we lose is a map to the world in its creation and its becoming—the whole story of why we are here at all. Words cannot replace the map of creation. They also cannot replace living human beings if we decide to erase the image of God in this world by annihilating each other. The created world is old, and everything in it still hums of mystery. The question is—as it always has been—whether we can hear it.

CHAPTER SEVEN

Beyond the Visible

Loving Witness in Daniel Clowes's *Wilson* and
Richard McGuire's *Here*

*Love lets the beloved appear in a glow that nobody else
perceives.*
—Robert Spaemann

*Through every human being, unique space, intimate space,
opens up to the world.*
—R. M. Rilke

Readers who have come with me this far might find it odd that I persist in describing the aesthetic attention paid by a writer to a character theologically, as an act of love. This is especially odd given my insistence (following Aquinas) that love is best defined as desiring the good for someone rather than simply having feelings for them.[1] In a way there is nobody less real than a character on a page, no matter how much the character may resemble an actual person. We certainly cannot desire the good life for a person who does not exist.

But it is equally true that love for any particular person must begin with the ability to see that person as worthy of love. This is why the philosopher Robert Spaemann devoted his career to the difficult ethical question of how to recognize and care for other persons, particularly

125

those our culture sees as expendable. In order to define love as a responsibility that goes beyond sentiment or empathy, Spaemann argues that love sees the other person as "just as real as we are."[2] Love sees beyond the person's qualities, and is committed to that person unconditionally. He quotes Richard of St. Victor: *Ubi amor, ibi oculus*—"Where love is, there is the eye."[3] Richard explodes the cliché "beauty is in the eye of the beholder" by his startling formulation. Loving and seeing are on a simultaneous footing, as if to see is to love and to love is to see. But how exactly does love see the other? As someone in possession of certain admirable qualities? No. Love sees the other as someone who possesses the same "incomparable uniqueness," and therefore inherent dignity, that the seer herself does.[4] This precisely does *not* mean that we see something of ourselves in the other in a way that produces empathy, though it might begin there. It means moving beyond emotion to recognition of the other as a member of the human community, as a *person* made in the image of God. Human beings as human beings "may be more or less similar; but as persons they are not similar, but equal— equal in their distinctive uniqueness and incommensurable dignity."[5]

It has been my contention throughout this book that aesthetic attention usually cultivates a loving vision because wherever the artist looks, she recognizes (and imparts) dignity and value. This is why I have persisted in arguing that the artist resembles God not in being a creator but in looking on the creation and calling it good, regardless of how badly broken it may be. In this light, a contemporary novelist succeeds in getting us to pay attention to her story by making her characters more real, not less. She loves the characters she talks about precisely insofar as they are like no one else but could be anyone. Aesthetic attention is thus a uniquely powerful kind of love: "Nicolás Gómez Dávila writes: 'To love someone means to understand the reason that God had to create this person.' It is in this sense that love gives sight. *Ubi amor, ibi oculus*. Love lets the beloved appear in a glow that nobody else perceives."[6]

When it comes to the ever-changing art of the novel, it is particularly apt today to speak of glowing. We are in the midst of the meteoric rise of a relatively new genre: the graphic novel.[7] Joining images and narrative in fresh and exciting ways, graphic novels pay a different kind of aesthetic attention to characters that goes beyond the constraints of the novel and the cinema to a powerful hybrid of both. Matt Madden's groundbreaking *99 Ways to Tell a Story* displays that power. It presents the very simplest of stories—a man who gets up and can't remember why he went to the refrigerator—in 99 different graphic modes.[8] The graphic novel has a unique ability to defamiliarize what we think we already know, making it an example of a classic definition of what we mean by the word *literature*.[9]

Two recent graphic novels that pursue these advantages especially creatively are Daniel Clowes's *Wilson* and Richard McGuire's *Here*. On the face of things, the two novels could not be more different. *Wilson* is a series of comic panels that trace one man's story over a few years. It contains a lot of text and a conventional, discernible plot. *Here* takes place over billions of years and the course of several different people's lives. It contains very little text, and no singularly discernible plot. Though *Wilson* is united by one particular character and *Here* by one particular place, both authors let ordinary human life appear in a glow that nobody else would otherwise perceive. Their work turns readers into self-conscious witnesses to an authorial love for all persons as unique and irreplaceable.

For the Love of Wilson

While Daniel Clowes has been writing comics for a number of years, *Wilson* is his first nonserialized graphic novel (fig. 7.1).[10] Published in 2010, it has played a prominent role in the ascendency of this new art form, and with good reason. *Wilson* reveals that there are some things that only a graphic novel can do, especially when it comes to point of view. But for all its ingenuity—and perhaps in order to highlight that ingenuity—*Wilson* mostly follows a fairly conventional story line. The protagonist is, like Roth's Everyman, a middle-aged, white, divorced male living in a suburban neighborhood. He's living in a narcissistic despair that doesn't recognize itself, an all too familiar American version of Kierkegaard's sickness unto death. One day it occurs to him that he hasn't called his father in a while and might regret that, so he calls him, only to discover that his father is ill. He soon dies, filling Wilson with a longing to reach out to his ex-wife, Pippi. He finds her and

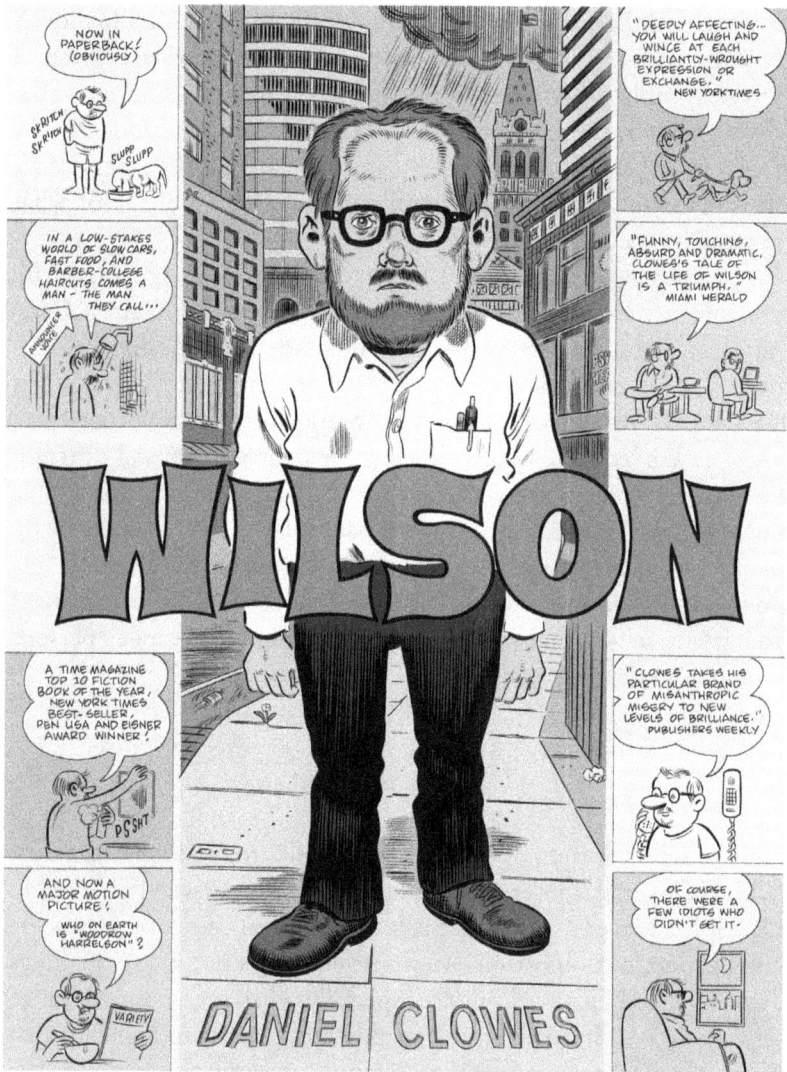

Figure 7.1. Wilson by Daniel Clowes, paperback cover. Reprinted with permission.

discovers she had given up a daughter for adoption who is probably (but not necessarily) his child. He hires someone to locate the now-teenaged daughter. They locate her and eventually Wilson tries to get the three of them to become a family. The rest of the story plays from there.

As with most films and plays, the storyteller of a typical graphic novel is neither seen nor heard. The storyteller is, instead, most in line with the implied author or focalizer—the one staging the character and the events for us to see and hear. While typically the implied author's vision remains consistent throughout, lending an air of objectivity, *Wilson* pushes against that. It consists of seventy pages, each a slice of the protagonist's life, but each of these pages is quite different from the others. Wilson is drawn in more than ten different variations, and the pages have coloring and other aesthetic choices unique to each.[11] The effect is unsettling but not in the way that typical unreliable narrative is unsettling. We know that when Edgar Allan Poe's narrator begins, "True!—nervous—very, very dreadfully nervous I had been and am; but why will you say that I am mad?," we cannot expect to get the truth. With *Wilson*, the differences in the drawings do not question the objectivity of events displayed but instead highlight the subjectivity inherent in an artist's visual interpretation of them. Clowes reminds us that artists are always choosing how to depict a character, how to represent what they witness. He reminds us that we see people in a variety of ways, too, and inevitably subjectively.

Clowes's particular visual variation strategy has other consequences for the reader's encounter with Wilson. First, the discontinuity of images highlights the strong continuity of Wilson's voice, which becomes his defining feature. Wilson is a delusional blowhard who speaks everything he thinks out loud, even while he repeatedly blames others for doing so. He verbally assaults strangers, often cursing loudly in their faces. The page "Cute Dog" is typical (fig. 7.2). More often than not, Clowes gives Wilson the verbal punch line in the last panel of the page, emphasizing how violently Wilson seizes for himself the last word. Since the verbal continuity is stronger than the visual, readers depend on it as we get to know Wilson—not unlike how playgoers depend on the continuity in Lear's speech to learn about him, even through thousands of different embodiments of his character. Wilson's

Figure 7.2. "Cute Dog." *Wilson* by Daniel Clowes. Reprinted with permission.

problems are beyond mere fatal flaw. What we learn from his speech is that he's as unlovable a protagonist as we will ever meet: a megalomaniacal and judgmental asshole living at the center of his own universe. But any way you draw him up, Wilson's voice is undeniably his own. As a result, *Wilson* is the perfect example of Peter Boxall's argument that voice in the novel persists as a kind of humanistic backlash against theory's effort to erase the self.[12]

Clowes's variations of Wilson's physical form also push the reader back and forth between the humor and the pathos of this character. A page drawn more comically puts more distance between us and an obviously fatuous and immature Wilson than does the more detailed and almost photolike drawings of his person. In "Fat Chicks," Wilson is short and round with beady eyes and a clownlike phallic nose, and we see him verbally judging women who walk by (fig. 7.3). Just one page over, in "Bad News," Clowes chooses the most realistic Wilson rendition to match the much more serious scene: Wilson finally manages to call his father, only to discover he has been ill for some time. The variations, coupled with the time gaps between pages, affords Clowes surprising emotional power and control. In "Deathbed," where the more realistically drawn Wilson is by his father's side, Wilson begs his unconscious father to talk to him about something real. "Come on, old man—I've been waiting 43 years to hear you say something honest and heartfelt and truthful to me." He gets no answer, which elicits his typical last-word panel response: "Come on, fucker!!" (26) (fig. 7.4). This page is followed immediately by "The Old Neighborhood," in which a smaller, rounder, and more caricatured Wilson is walking around where he grew up. Since we have been trained to view these scenes more comically, it is completely unexpected and disorienting when Wilson drops down on the pitcher's mound and says, "oh daddy daddy daddy" (fig. 7.5). Clowes's choice of the caricatured Wilson here works actively against a sentimental reading; he pushes us as far away from having sympathy for Wilson as possible.

The unique form of the graphic novel also cultivates this distance. As Scott McCloud has argued, comics, unlike any other art form, rely on the reader to provide closure between panels, to make guesses about what happens between them. Clowes relies on closure to draw us in and then push us away—just like Wilson does with the people in his

Figure 7.3. "Fat Chicks." *Wilson* by Daniel Clowes. Reprinted with permission.

Figure 7.4. "Deathbed." *Wilson* by Daniel Clowes. Reprinted with permission.

Figure 7.5. "The Old Neighborhood." *Wilson* by Daniel Clowes. Reprinted with permission.

own life, constantly baiting them to despise him. As if to maximize
the closure and drain out the emotional impact, Wilson's father dies
"offstage." After "The Old Neighborhood" we move directly to "All
Alone," in which Wilson, watching a father and daughter playing at a
park, begins to wonder if he should have been willing to make more
compromises with his ex-wife so that they could have had a family.
But Clowes stops the seriousness mid-speech; in the last panel Wilson
shouts, "Hey! Can you get that brat to shut up for two fucking seconds!?" (28). Empathy has once again been foreclosed.

Finally, and somewhat paradoxically, the variations of the forms
used to depict Wilson have the effect of highlighting his particularity.
As Hillary Chute argues, the visual medium of the graphic novel
provides writers a kind of "procedure of embodiment" that puts its
physicality front and center.[13] Although we are given different views
of Wilson's body, continuity overcomes disparity: we can't help but
collect the versions of him into something that we remember when we
think of the novel. This is a bit like how you might imagine Christian
Bale in your mind's eye right now, in spite of the different roles you
have watched him perform. In the "iconic solidarity" of this novel,
Wilson is clearly the same partly balding, middle-aged white man with
plastic frame eyeglasses.[14] Clowes reinforces this experience by drawing the most realistic version of Wilson in nearly a third of the novel's
pages. If McCloud is correct that artists draw characters more realistically when they want to emphasize their objective otherness from the
reader (as opposed to abstract characterizations that invite the reader's
identification), then Clowes's favoring of the realistic form has ethical
weight.[15] We recognize him as the particular and irreplaceable person
of "Wilson" in page after page, and we recognize him inside the particularity of his story. The titular Wilson *is* the story; there is no story
without him. Finally, by shifting his drawing styles, Clowes reminds
the reader that Wilson, like any well-conceived character, exceeds the
author's visualization of him. Although there is more to him than what
can be seen on any page, from any given point of view, Wilson remains,
as the back advertises, "100% Wilsonesque."

What does any of this have to do with love for persons? Like the
cinema and the theater, the graphic novel requires the indissoluble
union of the bodies and the souls of its characters.[16] It puts fully drawn,

ordinary people in our sight line. It accosts us with them. Clowes ironizes this fact with a strip on the back of the novel: Wilson is in a bookstore, declaring out loud, "all these books and not a single one about me!" Of course, the novel *is* about him. And the fact that a novel could be about such an ordinary Joe depends on a certain notion of the person, a notion that was introduced to western culture by Christianity. Emmanuel Mounier explains that although the concept was embryonic in antiquity, Christianity is what gives us the decisive notion of the person, a concept that was scandalous to ancient Greek thought.[17] "I am *a* being, in the *singular*, I have a *proper* name—a unity that is not the dead identity of a stone which is neither born, nor lives nor grows old." The person cannot be described in a formula because she is full of surprises born out of spontaneity. In short, a person is "irreplaceable in the position he occupies in the world of persons."[18]

Wilson is an irreplaceably particular person, and Clowes has managed to rivet our attention on him. Like Roth's Everyman, this is a remarkable achievement considering that Wilson is particularly unlikable, the sort of character who seems unredeemable. He mails a box of dog shit to his ex-wife's family. He accosts people in the airport and makes fun of their vocational choices. He's angry, and he blames everyone else for the way the world is. A particularly funny example of this is "Agent of Change," where he confronts a driver who had simply asked him for directions and then proceeds to berate a woman for actually giving him the directions. That Wilson is unlikable only makes my case more strongly. As I mentioned in chapter 1, Bakhtin taught us that aesthetic attention is what imparts value to the character in an act of loving consummation of that character, not whether he or she is good or bad.[19]

All this makes even more sense when we consider that the human consequences for failing to love others is arguably the main theme of the novel. The first page in the novel, titled "Fellowship," makes this case (fig. 7.6). Readers meet Wilson in a pose favorable to him. He looks directly at us—one of the few panels that breaks the fourth wall—and declares, "I love people!" and "I'm a people person!," and sermonizes about how tragic it is that we have lost our connection with others. But we soon find out that Wilson's self-description is inaccurate, for such a connection is precisely what Wilson's narcissism and anger prevents. By the fourth panel he has cheerfully greeted a fellow dogwalker:

Figure 7.6. "Fellowship." *Wilson* by Daniel Clowes. Reprinted with permission.

"Hello, sister. How's life treating you?" Taking his gesture as kindness, she begins to tell him about her day. She is allowed three speech balloons before Wilson abruptly replies, in the page's final panel, "For the love of Christ, don't you ever shut up?" The entire novel is structured like this page. When Wilson is alone, he knows he needs to connect with others; when he is actually around them, he hurls insults. His basic lack of empathy creates most of the humor of the novel, such as in the panel "Haircut" when his barber gives him a dose of his own medicine. After Wilson explains how significant it is to him to have discovered he has a daughter, the barber changes the subject to the local baseball team.

So why tell *Wilson*'s story? This is the question that lies at the very center of my book. And the answer is the same as it was with Roth's Everyman. Wilson's particularity is our particularity, even while his foibles are as uniquely his as ours are ours.[20] Authorial attention paid to him forces us to consider the similarities instead of the differences, just as Cormac McCarthy does when his narrator addresses the audience regarding his psychopathic character, Lester Ballard, who is a "child of God much like yourself perhaps."[21] Even the most narcissistic, broken, and despairing among us tries to connect with others, and wants to see deeper into the mystery of the interpersonal relationships that make us who we are. Clowes highlights this longing by depicting Wilson's search for an epiphany about his life, symbolically connected by images of water. The third page of the novel—"Mother"—is the first page in which Wilson is depicted very realistically as he walks around Oakland at night. Talking aloud with no one around (a common practice for him), he remembers the death of his mother. "She was so sick . . . it was actually kind of a relief at first. But then . . . it was like . . . like what if I told you tomorrow you'll never see the ocean again?" (9). Three pages later we see him sitting by the ocean and reflecting that his parents used to find "some kind of spiritual replenishment" by sitting there and "maybe they were trying to connect with something bigger, something vast and everlasting" (12). In *Civilization and Its Discontents*, Freud described this desire to be connected to everything as an "oceanic feeling" that he argues is ultimately just an illusion. Wilson would clearly like to believe the mystic's view of the world and feel it as unified in its significance, but he cannot access it. "I feel like if I sit here long enough, it will come to me. I feel like I'm on the verge of a profound personal breakthrough!" The next panel depicts him sitting there, waiting for the epiphany. He doesn't wait very long, however. The next panel shows him heading in the other direction declaring, "fuck it, this is a snooze-fest." In spite of his impatience, Wilson doesn't stop looking. We see him gazing at ice in the prison yard, rain on the windows. Will his epiphany ever come?

Keep reading to find out. But note that Clowes does not need to actually give Wilson an epiphany of this sort for me to make my case. Framing Wilson's experience in a book has already revealed Clowes's love for his character that speaks to the intersubjectivity of being and the continuity of human experience. Our interest in the novel cannot be fully explained without this kind of connection, as I have been arguing throughout. Clowes gives us a bit more to chew on, however. In his effort to rebuild his family, Wilson takes his ex-wife and daughter to a hotel and begins making plans for their future. His wife is not on board with his plans, so she calls the police, and Wilson is sent to prison for kidnapping. Six years go by in five pages, and Wilson seems completely unchanged and unfazed by his prison experience. When he is released, he tries to find his dog, and ends up in a passionless relationship with his former dog sitter. After an indeterminate amount of time passes, his daughter reaches out to him to tell him that she has married, moved to Alaska, and has a son of her own named Jason. Wilson's response is typically insensitive (prison hasn't helped at all!), and he shows only casual interest in her story of how much therapy she has had to undergo to deal with her childhood. In his characteristically self-centered way he suddenly blurts out, "Hey wait a minute! Jason is my grandson!"

This information works on Wilson for the next few pages. Eventually he pleads with his daughter to let him move to Alaska, and there is no indication that he is not serious about this. She wisely refuses. But near the end of the novel we get "iChat," which might be the book's most earnest and revelatory page (fig. 7.7). The first panel is reminiscent of the book's opening panel, in that Wilson seems to be looking right out at us, this time with a distressed look on his face. We quickly discover that he's not looking at us but into a computer screen. He says, "Hi Jason. It's Grandpa Wilson." The next panel shows Jason behaving

Figure 7.7. "iChat." *Wilson* by Daniel Clowes. Reprinted with permission.

the way any child would in this situation, confronted with a relative who has had no significance to him prior to this point: "it doesn't look like Grampa." Off screen his mother replies, "That's a new Grandpa." With a tear running down his cheek, Wilson tells Jason that he wants to visit him in Alaska. Jason, however, is as indifferent as any child would be in this situation; he wants to get off the chat and go back to playing. Wilson, now desperate, lifts a Thomas the Tank Engine toy. The reader sees something we had never seen in Wilson prior to this point: he has changed. He had researched the toy that Claire had mentioned earlier (that he was listening to her at all is no small thing), and he purchased it. The final panel depicts Wilson in a moment of significant intimacy and vulnerability.

Since we have been trained by the novel to expect comic relief immediately after any emotionally weighty scene, we are not surprised to see that the next page depicts Wilson in the same café where we've seen him verbally accost others. He again foists himself and his views on an unsuspecting fellow customer. "What's it going to be like for the kids of today?," he begins, and we learn that Wilson is the same narcissistic guy who is still not interested in an actual dialogue. But we also see him (possibly) in the process of changing his mind. "We like our stories to end with a promise of hope—'happily ever after' and all that. Too bad real lives don't have that structure," he says in one frame, then in the next, "Or hell, maybe they do. Maybe it's right there in front of us and we can't see it." He sighs, then says he's sick of feeling this way. The page ends with him on his feet with his hands in the air declaring, "I am a beautiful creature! I'm a living monument to nature's genius! I'm alive and breathing and strong! I'm a father! A grandfather! A million-in-one fucking miracle!" (76). The page, which is the novel's penultimate, ends with this proclamation.

Just as readers are left wondering how seriously to take it, our eyes are drawn to the final page of the novel (which, significantly, appears on the opposite page of the same spread): "Raindrop" (77) (fig. 7.8). Wilson is staring out the window at the rain. Apparently he has just had the epiphany he has been searching for, indicated by a large exclamation point. In the second panel he declares "Finally!," followed in the next frame by, "It's so obvious in a way, but it never even occured [sic] to me!" Exactly what has occurred to him, he doesn't say. But for

Figure 7.8. "Raindrop." *Wilson* by Daniel Clowes. Reprinted with permission.

a character who blurts out everything, the fact that he cannot articulate it in words is the most important thing about it. He sees something that we cannot really see and he cannot really say. The point of view pulls away from him sitting in front of the window, left with his thoughts.

Readers of novels are familiar with epiphany, a mainstay of the genre since its birth. Literary scholars have spent hours mapping its appearance and disappearance. It is possible that Clowes means for Wilson's epiphany to be ironic and that he wants us to walk away from the book without much hope for Wilson to be any different from the ignoble clod we have followed all along. Even if that were the case, there are two things that are not ironized here. The first is Wilson's discovery of himself as a father and a grandfather, and how that is linked to his desire for an epiphany. Since Wilson's desire is shaped by his feelings of isolation and insignificance, his searching takes the natural direction of connecting with others. It is telling that in Jean-Luc Marion's extensive development of the phenomenology of givenness, one of his primary examples of a phenomenon that has been reduced to givenness — that is, a phenomenon that cannot be converted from a gift into an object with mere exchange value — is fatherhood.[22] In phenomenological terms, by discovering he is a father and grandfather, Wilson has been given a window into the irreducible givenness of life itself. If I had to guess the content of Wilson's epiphany, this would be my guess.

Second, and even more important than Wilson's desire for a deeper meaning to his life, is Clowes's response to Wilson's desire. For even at the very moment Wilson states, "It's too bad real lives don't have that structure," Clowes reveals that Wilson's life *does* have a structure but that Wilson cannot see it from the inside. What is required is the viewpoint of the other, the outside, aesthetic perspective on his life — as everyday and quotidian as it clearly is. What is also required is that persons are revealed to possess the freedom to grow, change, be different.[23] What is required, in short, is the genre of the novel. Fiction, argues Gabriel Marcel, says, "I affirm you as being," and desires that persons, so wonderful as we have been made to be, should be eternal.[24] Even this formulation is too subjective, he notes, for it is not the affirmation of the value that gives the value but being itself. The affirmation of being becomes love when it "resigns itself in favor" of that being having value *in and of itself*. It takes faith to affirm the inherent dignity and value of persons.[25] That faith is the novelist's.

THE GIFT OF *HERE*

The case for storytelling as demonstrating love for particular persons is easier to make with the conventional, epiphany-centered plot that we saw in *Wilson*. What about a novel that is more about a particular place than it is about a particular person? Wouldn't that push against the central thesis? To find out, we turn to Richard McGuire's graphic novel, *Here*.[26]

Here capitalizes on the graphic novel's unique potential like nothing else before it. Rather than a series of panels that move in a linear fashion following the life of a particular person, *Here* consists of full-spread panels centered on one particular location in Perth Amboy, New Jersey. Most of the novel is set inside, in a corner of a small house that was built on that spot in 1907, but it also moves back and forth through time, from 3,000,500,000 BCE through the year AD 22,175. Any given primary panel is arranged in a spread and dated; it dramatizes the movement through time by embedding other, smaller dated panels in it—an idea McGuire got when he first saw Microsoft Windows (fig. 7.9). *Here* thus weds the focalization of painting with the narrative suspense of a mystery novel or a staged drama. There is no central plot, but there are discernible mini-stories. There is no single protagonist, but there are several people whose lives we are led to follow.

McGuire's work, like a representational painting, ensures that the reader cannot abstract where "here" is, even while we are invited to see the similarities between this place and our own places. McGuire's "here" is, in fact, based on his childhood home. The novel's focal point (the majority of panels) is this home, a single-dwelling house built in front of a larger colonial mansion that is modeled on the Propriety House, the former home of William Franklin. The Propriety House is a bona fide historical landmark: it is the last standing colonial proprietary governor's house in America.[27] McGuire's focalization is thus itself a radical move; the colonial mansion appears but is not central. It cannot be seen on any page or in any window dated after 1907. It is referred to by the characters in only offhanded ways: "I think Ben Franklin once lived there or planted a cherry tree there or something." The

Figure 7.9. 1623, with 1957 and 1999 windows. *Here* by Richard McGuire. Reprinted with permission.

primary focal point is instead the smaller house that both could (and cannot) be anywhere; it's the standard American "little pink house" that John Mellencamp sang about. But it is also *this* house in *this* spot. Different families live in this particular house over the generations. We see wallpaper going up and coming down. We see Christmas trees in the corner. In a particularly lovely self-reflexive sequence at the beginning, we see a painting over the hearth in 1957—a painting that depicts the same view as the forest we see in 1623, on the very next page. We see into the forest, meeting some Native Americans, probably Lenape. We see a Victorian couple enjoying a picnic lunch on the lawn in 1870. We see parents telling the story of how they met in 1988. In short, this novel is about ordinary Americans (before and after "America"), not famous ones. The people are connected forever and only by a particular spot, whether they are aware of that connection or not.

While the fact that no one person's or family's story is highlighted might seem to work against the idea of the value of personal being as I have expressed it throughout this book, *Here*'s beauty and power is still best explained within this conception. If McGuire chose a landscape that was nothing but a ditch, there would be no (necessary) aesthetic interest generated. If McGuire chose a landscape that was particularly beautiful, the panels would function like Monet's paintings of haystacks, but the book could not be called a novel, for its aesthetic interest would be unrelated to storytelling. For *Here* to work as a novel, the point of view must return to the particular human beings who lived in this spot. And, indeed, for the majority of panels we are invited into the living room of someone's house. We see what happens there, and we want to know more. This kind of vision is not voyeuristic; we aren't salaciously consuming other persons. What could the purpose of being brought into this home be but to say that human lives are beautiful, meaningful, interesting, and valuable for their own sake? *Here* uniquely highlights our ordinary experiences of being here—and being home.

I believe that *Here* would not succeed if it were not the case that personal ontology is rooted in intersubjectivity, as I have argued throughout. For while the place provides aesthetic unity, attention is generated by the characters and the reader's interest in them. This is partly why the first spread (beyond the title pages), in 1957, shows a playpen in the very center, in the book's gutter, with a baby bottle on the sofa (fig. 7.10). There is no more conventional opening for a story than a birth. This year, 1957, is also McGuire's own birth year, reminding us that the artist was here—and might not have been!—though knowledge of that autobiographical connection is not necessary to enjoy this novel. What is necessary is recognizing that this particular place would not have meaning without persons.

Neither would it have meaning without the faculty that is unique to persons: memory. *Here* touches on the way we search for continuity and significance over time, the way we remember our lives and hope that they will be remembered by those we love. The first spread that contains text returns us to 1957 and highlights memory. A woman in a pink dress is in a purplish living room with her back turned to us and says, "Hmm . . . now why did I come in here again?" The very last spread returns to 1957 and shows the same woman picking up a book on the coffee table and saying, "Now I remember." These 1957 "bookend" spreads subtly draw our attention to the relationship between books and memory; the book the woman had been looking for is bright

Figure 7.10. Playpen and baby's bottle in 1957. *Here* by Richard McGuire. Reprinted with permission.

yellow, standing out against the purple theme of 1957. The symbolism is strong, but the moment is as simple and ordinary as they come.

The moments between the beginning and the end of *Here* range over many years, with the order of the scenes determined sometimes by theme and sometimes by mini-plot. In short, this book does not have a random form. In each case, the date is often indicated by a color scheme that unconsciously guides the reader into these different plots. The year 1957 is purple and pink—cool tones that contrast strongly with the warm yellow and green tones of 1989; 1957 and the early panels focus on young children; 1989 and the later panels reveal the same people when they are much older. Most of what we watch are little moments within these families: a father lifting a baby; people dancing; a man noting how the dog barks at the doorbell every time it rings. To emphasize this passing of time within one family, our first introduction to the yellow tones of 1989 is superimposed on the purple tones of 1957 and features a mini-story in which four older people are sharing a joke, which causes one man to choke and fall over (fig. 7.11). The joke and choke scene in 1989 takes place over nine consecutive spreads. We can easily follow it, even as we watch the background images go back in time between 8,000 BCE and 1783, before this house is built. The joke is about a doctor who tells his patient he has good news and bad news; the good, that he has twenty-four hours to live. "'That's the good news?! What's the bad news?!'" We have to turn another page for the punch line: "The doctor says, 'I should have told you yesterday.'"[28] This same sofa is where family photos are taken; we watch the children grow up. Later, in 2005, a dying man is set up in a sofa bed in the same spot where the crib had been, the joke had been told, and the photos were taken. So even though the book is mostly about "forgotten little things," McGuire manages to highlight the big things that mark human experience: death, memory, and the ephemerality of being.[29] He literally maps the littlest things in life onto the biggest things in life.[30]

Here is an astonishing accomplishment. It is so metaphysically dizzying that it is nearly impossible to understand how it works on

Figure 7.11. "Tell that joke about the doctor." *Here* by Richard McGuire. Reprinted with permission.

readers without recourse to ideas that go beyond this particular place—beyond the story. This is why I believe that the book that makes best sense of its power is a phenomenological one: Gaston Bachelard's *The Poetics of Space*. Although Bachelard explores images from conventional novels, graphic novels arguably make the case more poignantly. Bachelard argues that any time a novel presents an image of a house, it works powerfully on readers in unconscious ways. The house image has become "the topography of our intimate being."[31] This can only be the case, of course, because of the nature of personal being and consciousness. Because of the necessarily local and grounded way we experience the world, any given inhabited space "bears the essence of the notion of home."[32] As a result, house images powerfully integrate the "thoughts, memories and dreams of mankind."[33] They do this regardless of authorial intention.

Bachelard devotes a whole chapter to the phenomenology of corners, and another one to immensity. *Here* focuses on both. The gutter is aligned with a corner of the house, making that corner our focal point when we are inside the house. But in 3,000,500,000 BCE "here" is only a vast wash of sea and sky. The early spreads suggest the immensity of Genesis 1:2, in which the earth was formless and void and darkness was over the surface of the deep. In 2111, we see floodwaters pouring into the window when the Atlantic Ocean reclaims the Jersey shore (fig. 7.12). Life "here" is destroyed, and in 2313, becomes radioactive. But in the latest date of the book, 22,175, the spot is restored—vastly. Flora and fauna pop out with fluorescent green and pink, brighter colors than any others in the book (fig. 7.13). These paintings never cover more than half a spread, as if to say, "Here's a peek into the new world after this one is renewed." A new heaven and a new earth? Perhaps.

Regardless, McGuire's daydream of 22,175 makes perfect sense when considered in light of Bachelard's theories. Images of corners (retreat) and images of immensity (enlargement) are related to each other dialectically. They are the most psychically powerful images a novelist can employ. Bachelard describes how the writer Philippe Diolé exercised this dialectic when writing about the Sahara: "The *being-here* is maintained by a being from elsewhere. Space, vast space, is the friend of being."[34] Is there any other work of art that exercises that dialectic

Figure 7.12. Entropy. *Here* by Richard McGuire. Reprinted with permission.

Figure 7.13. Girl looking up chimney into AD 22,175. *Here* by Richard Mc-Guire. Reprinted with permission.

as effectively as *Here*? Figure 7.13 might be the book's most ambitious attempt to capture that dialectic and reveal how personal being is what holds it all together. A young girl in a pink dress looks up the chimney in 1935, but what we see there is the new world of AD 22,175. She has been playing with a doll house that reproduces the same corner of the house we have been looking at—complete with people, some wearing pink. These doll-people have dolls of their own. Furthermore, near the corner of the main house in 1935, there is a painting hanging on the wall, clearly Vermeer's *Woman in Blue Reading a Letter*.[35] In 2014, we see a large ear that belongs to someone closer to us than anyone else has been in the book. Listening, looking, reading, living. It is all symphonic. It is all here.

While it is tempting to think of the physical location as that which provides the unity of the novel, this spread helps us to understand why that is not the case. The house (meaningless without its inhabitants) is what provides it. McGuire could have been channeling Bachelard when he said of his childhood house, "I spent there many significant years, but at the end what really happens is that we take the house with us. I'm convinced of that. It's the idea of a home what's important. I often dream with that house."[36] For Bachelard, houses can never be neutral. They are always in our dreams; they hold us together psychically. Without the house, human being would be a "dispersed being." Human being begins in closed, protected, warm spaces. First the womb, then the cradle. "Before he is 'cast into the world,' as claimed by certain hasty metaphysics, man is laid in the cradle of the house. And always, in our daydreams, the house is a large cradle."[37] Human persons are born into well-being in a cosmos, not isolated in a universe.[38] The integrative force of the house is what keeps readers from feeling sad, even as we journey through McGuire's substantial nod to entropy and loss. Figure 7.12 is fragmented into frames featuring balloons with various insults as well as frames featuring things falling and breaking. Later, a five-panel sequence highlights a wide range of losses: "I lost my wallet"; "I think I'm losing my mind"; "I am losing my eyesight"; "Shit, I lost an earring" (fig. 7.14). Through entropy and loss, the here that is home holds it all together.

I have taught this book several times since it was published in its complete form in 2014. The most prominent response of my students

Figure 7.14. "I Lost my Wallet!" *Here* by Richard McGuire. Reprinted with permission.

to the question of its meaning is to say that *Here* is a gift because it powerfully speaks to the here and now of all of our lives as a gift. This same insight is what leads Paul Gravett to praise the novel, writing, "Seldom has the relativity of time and of our own place within it been expressed so elegantly or emotionally. The real wonder is that any of us are 'here' at all."[39] That this is a decisively theological interpretation explains why I am ending my project *Here*. In the *Mystery of the Supernatural*, Henri de Lubac argues that humans are driven to seek beatitude. Following Saint Thomas, he insists that the desire to see God is "inscribed upon my very being." But the desire for God remains latent in human beings until we experience a universal, existential, and inevitable moment: the moment we look at our individual lives and see that what had a beginning will also have an end. We learn from our finitude what only our finitude can teach us, that we have received the gift of being. This gift is radical. It is incomparably better than any other gift we could receive.[40]

Because *Here* is a window open to the metaphysical structure of being itself as a gift, it is remarkably beautiful. Like Cormac McCarthy's *The Road*, it is under the demand of the beautiful, for to treat this subject as if it were ugly would be untrue to it. McGuire's decision to extend into a novel what had only appeared previously in smaller bits acquiesces to this idea. The move enabled him to treat each spread as a separate painting, to elevate his simple subject into the canon of great works of art. With its thick, high-quality paper and overall heft, the book is much closer to an art book than it is to its comic book precursors, leading Rachel Cooke to proclaim that it is an "exquisitely drawn book, its restrained palette and pop style calling to mind the work of such diverse artists as Vermeer, Vilhelm Hammershoi and Richard Hamilton. To hold it is to covet it."[41]

To hold *Here* in your hands can be a profoundly theological experience. Because of this artist's accomplishment, we are able to take a tiny corner of space and a big swath of time and hold it in our hands, to peer into the human and creaturely life that inhabited it, to have access to the future, which is also strangely present. If that sounds familiar, it is because it is the way that Christians have long understood that God sees creation, the kind of loving, grace-saturated valuation of us in the here and now. God holds us in his hands.

It is therefore no surprise that the closest analogue to McGuire's aesthetic vision would be from a Christian mystic who lived many years ago: Julian of Norwich.

> Also in this revelation He showed a little thing, the size of a hazel nut in the palm of my hand, and it was as round as a ball. I looked at it with the eye of my understanding and thought: "What can this be?" And it was generally answered thus: "It is all that is made."
>
> I marveled how it could continue, because it seemed to me it could suddenly have sunk into nothingness because of its littleness. And I was answered in my understanding: "It continueth and always shall, because God loveth it; and in this way everything hath its being by the love of God."[42]

Julian's eyes are the eyes of the artist. Whether she knows it or not, the artist consults God in looking at things. That look is a look of love.

NOTES

Introduction

1. D'Souza and Seiling, *Being in the World*, 26. Jens Zimmermann puts it this way: "Artistic expression, whether explicitly religious or secular, always constitutes a human interpretation of the world that beholds objects as participating in the mystery of being." Zimmermann, *Incarnational Humanism*, 290.

2. Dennett, *Breaking the Spell: Religion as a Natural Phenomenon*.

3. Degler, *In Search of Human Nature*, viii.

4. Wilson, *Sociobiology*, 4.

5. Dissanayake, *What Is Art For?*; Dutton, *The Art Instinct*; Gottschall, *The Storytelling Animal*. As Dissanayake puts it in a later book, "Whereas it is usual to think of human nature as being the product of gods, societies, and cultures, the species-centric position takes the reverse view: it holds that gods, societies, and cultures are the products, the answers, and embodiments of the species needs and potentials of an already existing human nature. Having recognized this truth, one can then go on, if one desires, to examine and understand cultural differences." Dissanayake, *Homo Aestheticus*, 5.

6. See Baker, *Naturalism and the First-Person Perspective*.

7. The issue of what animals can and cannot do is too complex to be treated fully here. For example, elephants appear to paint, but closer inquiry indicates that they have been trained to make the marks on the canvas; they did not generate the mimetic activity. See Morris, "Can Jumbo Elephants Really Paint?" Gorilla language acquisition, as I discuss in chapter 5, is a trickier question. But my argument in this book does not depend on a rigid animal vs. human binary. I agree with Robert Spaemann, who ended his most important treatment of the rights of persons with these lines: "The rights of persons are human rights. Yet if there exist within the universe other natural species of living beings possessing an inner life of sentience, whose adult members usually command rationality and self-awareness, we would have to acknowledge *not only those instances but all instances* of that species to be persons. All porpoises, for example." Spaemann, *Persons: The Difference between "Someone" and "Something,"* 248;

original emphasis. At the very least, we know enough about the possibility of gorilla self-awareness to merit them the dignity of being left alone.

8. Damasio, *Self Comes to Mind*, 18.

9. Damasio deals with the problem of qualia in a chapter titled "Putting It Together." He argues that the question of why our experiences in the world should feel like anything calls for evolutionary reasoning. "If perceptual maps of the body are to be effective in leading an organism toward avoidance of pain and seeking of pleasure, they should not only feel like something, they actually *ought* to feel like something. The neural construction of pain and pleasure states must have been arrived at early in evolution and must have played a critical role in its course." *Self Comes to Mind*, 275. Of course, the *ought* does not necessitate the *is*. It would be just as easy to make the argument that any given species would be likely to have better survival rates if it never had the capacity to feel anything that would make them second guess their own actions. The best explanation for the kind of reasoning that eliminative materialism requires is from Thomas Nagel, who called it "Darwinism of the gaps." Nagel, *Mind and Cosmos*.

10. In addition to *Consciousness Explained*, see Dennett's TED talk, www.ted.com/talks/dan_dennett_on_our_consciousness.

11. Daniel Dennett argues, "Let me put the problem unequivocally: the traditional concept of the soul as an immaterial thinking thing, Descartes's *res cogitans*, the internal locus in each human body of all suffering, and meaning, and decisions, both moral and immoral, has been utterly discredited. Science has banished the soul as firmly as it has banished mermaids, unicorns, and perpetual motion machines." Dennett, "How to Protect Human Dignity from Science," 44.

12. An interesting example of how this conflict operates can be seen in Jonathan Gottschall's critique of Naomi Wolf's *The Beauty Myth*. Wolf's book is an exemplary expression of the cultural constructivist position; Gottschall collects and crunches data from stories around the world. The data reveal that stories told within every human culture favor characters that exhibit physical beauty, particularly in female characters. Since Wolf argues that female beauty is a Western construct, Gottschall believes he has disproven her argument. Responses to this argument followed, as would be expected, with most literary scholars still lining up on the constructivist side. Gottschall, *Literature, Science, and a New Humanities*, 127–56.

13. Taylor, *A Secular Age*, 59.

14. Kearney, *On Stories*, 3.

15. Michael Ruse argues that Darwinian evolution has always positioned itself as an alternative to Christianity: "Christianity and Darwinism are rivals, different reflections of the same reality." Literary fiction is one of the key battlegrounds for these competing metanarratives. "Making the crucial distinctions between pseudoscience and popular science, and popular science and professional science, it was at the popular science level that Darwinism struck hardest and had the greatest effect. And seen in this light, there was something we can properly speak of not just as a revolution in science but as a religious revolution, whether you want to speak without qualification of Darwinism as a religion or

more cautiously of Darwinism as offering a new, secular religious perspective." Ruse, *Darwinism as Religion*, 194, 281.

16. Taliaferro, *The Golden Cord*, 68. Taliaferro's book was one of the early inspirations for this project.

17. As Jens Zimmermann has argued, when the incarnation has its rightful place in Christian theology, it teaches a participatory logic regarding the relationship between human beings and reality. Human beings were made to see Jesus at the center of creation. Zimmermann, *Incarnational Humanism*, 52–113.

18. This astonishment is one I share with Marilynne Robinson. Robinson, *Absence of Mind*, 32–33. In a later essay "Humanism," Robinson singles out the discipline of neuroscience for its unwillingness to recognize how its starting assumptions dictate its conclusions: "The gist of neuroscience is that the adverbs 'simply' and 'merely' can exorcise the mystifications that have always surrounded the operations of the mind/brain, exposing the machinery that in fact produces emotion, behavior, and all the rest." Robinson, *The Givenness of Things*, 6.

19. Kearney, *On Stories*, 5; original emphasis.

20. Hart, *The Experience of God*.

21. I use the word *love* because, unfortunately, there is no better word in English to describe what I mean. As many writers have noted, in the English language the word has serious limitations. Robert Spaemann argues that "there is no word—except maybe 'freedom'—that has such a wide-ranging and often contradictory conglomerate of meanings as the word 'love.'" Spaemann, *Love and the Dignity of Human Life*, 2. Along with Spaemann, I define love not as a feeling but as a habit, a way of thinking and acting toward another person. I also prefer the definition provided by St. Thomas Aquinas: "an act of love always tends towards two things; to the good that one wills, and to the person for whom one wills it: since to love a person is to wish that person good." Aquinas, *Summa Theologica* 1.20.1.

22. As far as we know right now this robust first-person consciousness is uniquely human, but my argument does not de facto preclude the possibility that other species could be discovered to possess it. If they did possess it, they would, too, be storytelling animals.

23. This idea reveals the influence, especially in the West, of the Judeo-Christian idea of the person. See Taylor, *Sources of the Self*.

24. By "incarnational," I mean that the artist starts with the physical world that he or she believes to be good and, thereby, revelatory of the creator. This does not mean that everything in the world is sacred.

25. Hubert Dreyfus and Sean Dorrance Kelly argue that the "whooshing up" experience is premodern, necessarily temporary, and pretty much all we have of the sacred in today's society. "What there really is, for Homer, is whooshing up: the whooshing up of shining Achilles in the midst of battle, or of an overwhelming eroticism in the presence of a radiant stranger like Paris; the whooshing up of a rock in the turbulent sea that calls forth Odysseus's hand to grab it. These were the shining moments of reality in Homer's world. And whooshing up is what happens in the context of the great moment in contemporary sport as

well. When something whooshes up it focuses and organizes everything around it." Dreyfus and Kelly, *All Things Shining*, 200–201. Amy Hungerford argues that contemporary American literature operates much the same way; it provides a religious feeling of belief as a substitute for any meaningful object of belief. Hungerford, *Postmodern Belief.*

26. As we shall see, Hans Urs von Balthasar insisted that there can be no art for art's sake. Balthasar, *The Glory of the Lord*. Similarly, Hart argues that beauty is "the startling reminder, even for persons sunk in the superstitions of materialism, that those who see reality in purely mechanistic terms do not see the real world at all, but only its shadow." Hart, *The Experience of God*, 284.

27. Irenaeus continues that the life of the human being "consists in behold-ing God." "Against Heresies" 4.20.7. Roberts, *The Ante-Nicene Fathers.*

ONE.   Beyond the Author

1. Tomasello, *Constructing a Language*, 22. Charles Taylor explains that this "intense common focus" is the "crucial difference which sets humans off on the road to language" and rapid cultural evolution. Taylor, *The Language Animal*, 56. I treat this difference more closely in chapter 4.

2. This would be true even if the only other reader was the writer's future self.

3. Knapp and Michaels, "Against Theory."

4. It is not my intent to get into the tricky issues of artificial intelligence (AI) here. I will point out, however, that if the Turing test is what is used to fool someone into thinking that an AI is a person, all that has really been done is to acquiesce to a Cartesian definition of personhood in which cognition is valued over embodiment or the qualia that results therefrom. See Hayles, *How We Became Posthuman.*

5. Herman, *The Cambridge Companion to Narrative*, 9.

6. Phillips, *Ernest Hemingway on Writing*, 77.

7. Hutto, *Narrative and Understanding Persons.*

8. Bal, *Narratology*, 149. This is also what Kearney means when he argues that storytelling is "never neutral. Every narrative bears some evaluative charge regarding the events narrated and the actors featured in the narration." Kearney, *On Stories*, 155.

9. For a response to the argument that stories about fictional persons somehow lessen the ethical impact, see Dadlez and Haramia, "Fictional Objects, Future Objectives."

10. By "personalism," I am referring to a very loosely organized group of neo-Thomist philosophers, including Emanuel Mounier, Etienne Gilson, Ga-briel Marcel, and Jacques Maritain, who argued in a variety of different venues for the theological value of distinctive persons made in the image of God. This tradition continues with Henri de Lubac and Robert Spaemann, and in a slightly different form, with Hans urs von Balthasar. I should also note that important aspects of personalism continue today in the work of Jean-Luc Marion, who

writes about the dangers of objective definition. *"Defining a man always even-tually amounts to having done with the humanity in him, and thus to having done with him,"* he writes. "The abolition of man begins with his objectification, which itself consists in being able (believing oneself able) to define him without admitting the *who* within him." Marion and Lewis, *Negative Certainties*, 26–27; original emphasis. To see a person as something other than an object of knowl-edge and/or control requires that we see them as a mystery. "We vouch for our common humanity by each preserving the indefinition of the other: each safe-guards the incomprehensibility of the other by holding back his own gaze from reducing the other to the rank of a clear and distinct object" (37). Marion traces this idea, which is linked to the incomprehensibility of God and of humans made in God's image, to Gregory of Nyssa.

11. Mounier, *Personalism*, 35; original emphasis.

12. Barthes, *Image-Music-Text*, 160.

13. Ibid., 147.

14. Baker, *Naturalism and the First-Person Perspective*. Walker Percy ex-plains that the word *conscious* means "knowing with" and requires intentional-ity. "Does this offer us a sort of clue for getting at consciousness as something besides a queer kind of ghost inhabiting a machine called a body?" Percy and Samway, *Signposts in a Strange Land*, 124.

15. Quoted in Welker, *The Depth of the Human Person*, 15.

16. Baker, *Naturalism and the First-Person Perspective*, 77.

17. Ibid., 101; original emphasis.

18. Ibid., 140.

19. Ricoeur, *Oneself as Another*, 33.

20. "The novelist has isolated himself. The birthplace of the novel is the solitary individual, who is no longer able to express himself by giving examples of his most important concerns, is himself uncounseled, and cannot counsel others." Benjamin, *Illuminations*, 87.

21. Derek Attridge, whose book, regrettably, I discovered and read only very late in the completion of this one, calls the literary work an *event* (because it requires an audience or it would otherwise be lost) that has *singularity*. "The singularity of a cultural object consists in its difference from all other such ob-jects, not simply as a particular manifestation of general rules but as a peculiar nexus within the culture that is perceived as resisting or exceeding all pre-existing general determinations. Singularity, that is to say, is generated not by a core of irreducible materiality or vein of sheer contingency to which the cultural frame-works we use cannot penetrate but by a configuration of general properties that, in constituting the entity (as it exists in a particular time and place), goes beyond the possibilities pre-programmed by a culture's norms, the norms with which its members are familiar and through which most cultural products are under-stood." Attridge, *The Singularity of Literature*, 90–91. I have tended to alternate between "singularity" and "particularity" to describe the literary event, and my agreement with Attridge on this point is strong.

22. This might be the best place to indicate my departure from Attridge, who tends to follow Jacques Derrida's lead when it comes to questions of origins,

authorship, and otherness (which he usually calls alterity). Derrida bends away from the personal and the theological in his description of language-as-event; I contend that such cannot reasonably be done. Attridge's discussion of alterity, and the ethical responsibility thereto, feels depersonalized. See Attridge, *The Singularity of Literature*, ch. 9. As I try to argue throughout this book (without losing my readers in a philosophical jungle), the incarnation of Christ is what leads me to contend that standing with Gadamer, Bakhtin, Marcel, and Ricoeur is very different from standing with Derrida and Levinas when it comes to the question of answerability to art and the other.

23. Beyond the efforts of writers of metafiction, I cannot think of any American writers who deliberately try to be impersonal. If such a text exists, it would be an exception that proves the rule, and would still rely on readers who cannot cease to be persons.

24. Juster, *The Dot and the Line*. The film can be seen on YouTube at Charles Guajardo, *The Dot and the Line*.

25. It is worth noting that the depersonalized aspects of the poststructuralist theory of language can be traced to Maurice Blanchot, who took Mallarmé's view of poetic language as a kind of starting point. Speaking of Mallarmé, Blanchot writes, "The poetic word is no longer someone's word. In it no one speaks, and what speaks is not anyone. It seems rather that the word alone declares itself. Then language takes on all of its importance. It becomes essential. Language speaks as the essential, and that is why the word entrusted to the poet can be called the essential word. This means primarily that words, having the initiative, are not obliged to serve to designate anything or give voice to anyone, but that they have their ends in themselves." Blanchot, *The Space of Literature*, 41. My argument relies rather on M. M. Bakhtin's analysis of novelistic discourse for his insistence that no utterance can be ultimately severed from persons and personality. He writes that "there are no 'neutral' words and forms—words and forms that can belong to 'no one'; language has been completely taken over, shot through with intentions and accents. For any individual consciousness living in it, language is not an abstract system of normative forms but rather a concrete heteroglot conception of the world." Bakhtin, *The Dialogic Imagination*, 293. Poets working for abstraction have actively to suppress the fact that an utterance is always already peopled, starting with, of course, the author herself.

26. Barth, *Lost in the Funhouse*, 113.

27. Bakhtin's work is very important to my argument throughout this book. While I do not deal directly with questions of his personal faith, it will become clear that his view of aesthetic activity, with its insistence on "outsidedness," centers on the incarnation and is in clear defiance of Cartesian accounts of thinking. For a useful collection of essays that addresses these issues, see Felch and Contino, *Bakhtin and Religion*.

28. Bakhtin, *Art and Answerability*, 22.

29. Ibid., 35–36; original emphases.

30. Bakhtin, *Toward a Philosophy of the Act*, 62; original emphasis.

31. Maritain, *Person and the Common Good*, 28. It is important to note that my definition of love requires a respect for the otherness of the person. To want

the best for another requires that we know the other as other very well. Bakhtin's consummating consciousness would be reduced to an act of violence otherwise.

32. Of course, the unity of the three-in-one in God is very different from the unity of created persons who are invited into this perichoresis by way of Christ. As I show in my discussion of Toni Morrison's *Beloved*, love for human others requires this distinction.

33. Gunton, *The One, the Three and the Many*. Gunton makes it very clear that this is an ontological relationship involving a "dependence upon a God understood substantially and not abstractly" (194).

34. Sartre, *Nausea*, 39.

35. Ibid., 40.

36. Marcel, *Mystery of Being*, 2:153.

37. Dames, "The New Fiction of Solitude."

38. Dames suggests that the popularity of autofiction is due to the fact that we are so ultra-connected in our internet age that we need to rediscover how to be alone.

39. Taliaferro, *The Golden Cord*, 101.

40. de Lubac, *The Discovery of God*, 190.

41. Bakhtin, *Art and Answerability*, 111.

42. D'Souza and Seiling, *Being in the World*, 30. Also, art cannot but express "more than it is"; see Williams, *Grace and Necessity*, 60.

43. Williams, *Grace and Necessity*, 18; original emphasis.

44. Bakhtin, *Toward a Philosophy of the Act*, 62.

TWO.   Beyond the Self

1. Gogol, *Dead Souls*, 142–43.

2. One of Roth's earliest interviewers mentioned to him that "there were many things about it that struck me as having their roots in Russian literature. . . . I kept thinking of Dostoevsky, believe it or not, and Gogol, of course." Roth, *Conversations with Philip Roth*, 6.

3. Regarding Roth's narcissism, my favorite reflection is that of Wallace, "John Updike, Champion Literary Phallocrat, Drops One; Is This Finally the End for Magnificent Narcissists?"

4. *New York Times*, "What Is the Best Work of American Fiction of the Last 25 Years?" As many have noted, the methodology of the informal survey led to some misleading results.

5. Krasnik, "'It No Longer Feels a Great Injustice That I Have to Die'"; CBS News, "Philip Roth on Fame, Sex and God."

6. Hungerford, *Postmodern Belief*, 137. Patrick Hayes also describes Roth as having resolutely secular, Nietzschean goals: "Refusing the 'heartening and reassuring' sound of ethics talk, Roth suggests that literature of the highest stature explores life in an extra-moral way through a fascinated delight in 'power-seeking,' which it incarnates in its own potent linguistic effects." Hayes, *Philip Roth*, 3.

7. Roth, *Everyman*, 14. Subsequent references to this novel are indicated parenthetically.

8. My reading stands in stark contrast to that of Ben Schermbrucker, for example, who writes, "Everyman desires to write an autobiography called *The Life and Death of a Male Body* (52). Of course, his desire to write such an autobiography is subject to the meta-textual irony that Roth, in *his* novel, is doing just that." Schermbrucker, "'There's No Remaking Reality,'" 42. Throughout this book my argument hinges on the difference between trying to give one's own life this meaning as opposed to the outsidedness of the author (and, ultimately, of God) providing and acknowledging it.

9. Except for Philip Roth himself, who far too often is his own subject, a problem I address at the end of this chapter.

10. It is interesting that Mark Shechner, who tries to explain his enduring interest in Roth, noted that Roth's earlier novel *The Counterpoint* too far eroded the self/other relationship that I am arguing is the core of a good novel and ended up presenting the reader with "a hall of mirrors." Shechner, *Up Society's Ass, Copper*, 80.

11. In the logic of my argument, the only way a writer could avoid inherently valuing human life would be either to celebrate the character's degradation or not to bear witness at all. It is, therefore, quite interesting that after he published *Nemesis*, Roth declared that he was no longer interested in writing novels. If indeed one's life can be reduced to "the life and death of a male body," this is a reasonable decision. Flood, "Philip Roth Insists 'I Have No Desire to Write Fiction.'"

12. O'Connor, *Mystery and Manners*, 115. Thus *Everyman* is dialogic, as Bakhtin illustrated the novel necessarily is. See Bakhtin, *The Dialogic Imagination*. Tim Parks argues that Roth is an "unashamedly didactic" writer and that "at no point is any character allowed to challenge Roth's scheme." Parks, *Life and Work*, 151–52. If Bakhtin is correct, however, then the characters do challenge the scheme simply by their existence as characters with voices and choices.

13. Of course, as a fictional character she makes no actual choices, but Dreiser did not depict her as an automaton or mentally disabled in any way.

14. Marcel argues that it is a mistake to think of freedom in terms of causality: "I would readily agree that it is meaningless from the point of view of determinism, just as there would be no significance in trying to find a bond of cause and effect between the successive notes of a melody." Marcel, *Mystery of Being*, 2:113. This fascinating analogy shows how Marcel believes that the materialistic discussion regarding free will has lost the forest of personhood for the trees of individual actions.

15. Ibid., 114.

16. Ibid.

17. As I hope to make clear, it is not the simple fact of autobiographical elements that makes the novel feel narcissistic. Roth correctly assesses that *Portnoy's Complaint* was such a scandalous hit primarily because readers could not understand that it was not autobiography and was never intended to be. His "novel in the guise of a confession" was misread by readers "as a confession in

the guise of a novel." This move forgets the work as work and plagued Roth throughout his career. Roth, *Reading Myself and Others*, 254.

18. Wallace, "John Updike, Champion Literary Phallocrat, Drops One; Is This Finally the End for Magnificent Narcissists?"

19. Lezard, "*Nemesis* by Philip Roth—Review."

20. Bakhtin, *Art and Answerability*, 111–12.

21. Roth, *The Counterlife*.

22. Ibid., 320. Part of the reason that *The Counterlife* is so important to the "outsidedness" issue is that it is a Zuckerman novel, and those novels were both the most autobiographical of Roth's works and the ones in which he advanced his theories of the self as an impersonation. As Pia Masiero writes, "Zuckerman's is the self that helps Roth the most in getting himself through; it is the cornerstone in the construction of 'Philip Roth.'" Masiero, *Philip Roth and the Zuckerman Books*, 4. With regard to the self as joke, see Posnock, *Philip Roth's Rude Truth*.

23. James Duban engages the issue more directly in Duban, "From Negative Identity to Existential Nothingness." For Sartre, "Being-in-itself" means (very) roughly a thing as it is, its inert facticity; as opposed to "Being-for-itself," which is dynamically related to consciousness and transcendence. Humans possess both, but they doom us to a sense of alienation.

24. Marcel, *Mystery of Being*, 2:9–10.

25. Ibid., 175.

26. Since *American Pastoral* is one of the Zuckerman books, that may seem an odd claim. But the Zuckerman of Roth's best novels is a narrator of the experience of others, which Roth shows Zuckerman trying to work through and make sense of. *American Pastoral* is that kind of novel. The closer Zuckerman gets to Roth as disinterested novelist rather than Roth as anxious self-creator, the closer he gets to Bakhtinian aesthetic seeing.

27. In his review of *The Ghost Writer*, Jokinen writes, "This is Roth's great innovation, a character with a skill for Pre-emptive Self-recrimination: he gets away with murder because he admits to his crimes while he's committing them, and if you value honesty you got to love the guy, even if his honesty is crudely manipulative. He can do what he wants as long as he's not fooling himself into believing it's not wrong." Jokinen, "Last of the Great Male Narcissists?"

28. Kathy Knapp persuasively argues that *Everyman* can be seen as a part of a general post-9/11 re-vision of the suburban novel and its typical focus on middle-class male angst and tacit acceptance of American exceptionalism. The "ashes to ashes trajectory" that Everyman traces "brings to a self-conscious end the tradition of the everyman who stands in heroic opposition to society in a manner that only strengthens it by contributing to the mythos of the rugged individual." Knapp, *American Unexceptionalism*, xxxvii.

29. In a 1977 interview, Roth said the first-person point of view is "for me a way of gaining stylistic freedom. . . . And of course it's the 'I' who can be most *intimate*, who speaks in confidence, who tells us secrets—sexual secrets, hate secrets, love secrets, family secrets, tribal secrets, the stuff of shame, embarrassment, humiliation and disgrace." Roth, *Conversations with Philip Roth*, 104.

30. Ironically, the scene in Ezekiel ends up with God's promise of resurrection. "I will open your graves and raise you from your graves, O my people. And I will bring you into the land of Israel" (Ezek. 37:12).

31. D'Souza and Seiling, *Being in the World*, 209.

32. Ibid., 217.

33. Mounier, *Personalism*, 20.

34. As Spaemann argues, knowledge of the other tends to subsume the other, but as "Valentin Tornberg says: 'Love is the becoming real of the other for me.'" Spaemann, *Love and the Dignity of Human Life*, 19.

35. Jokinen, "Last of the Great Male Narcissists?"

36. Marion, *Negative Certainties*, 29. Ephraim Radner draws on Marion's work to argue that "death is the one event that most clearly divulges the creaturely miracle of our making." Radner, *A Time to Keep*, 154.

37. I agree with Liliana Naydan that the artistic impulse is more central in *Everyman* than most critics recognize. But Naydan argues that the novel offers art as a substitute for religious desire, not as an indicator of it. It attains "some semblance of transcendence" and offers an "art-based ideology" that can counter fundamentalist ideologies of all stripes, atheist and religious. Naydan, *Rhetorics of Religion in American Fiction*, 63–64.

38. Mounier, *Personalism*, 44. "The pressure of nature upon us and the labours by which we respond to it, are not merely factors making for productivity; they are also forces disruptive of egocentricity, and for that reason they are cultural and spiritual forces, quite as important as power or riches and doubtless more so. We must not, then, undervalue the external life: without it the inner life tends to insanity, as surely as the outer life becomes chaotic without interiorization."

39. Knapp concludes that this passage "eloquently rewrites the human equation: it is not a matter of having our individual worth recognized but of taking full measure of the invaluable, fragile world that surrounds us." Knapp, *American Unexceptionalism*, 109. This can be a conclusion only of the novelist who has left self-justification behind.

40. Though our approaches are a little different, Graham Ward also sees literature as resisting secularization because of moments like this one. All literature features "rhetorical and aesthetic attempts to tell it as it is: even if the 'truth' revealed is the brutish, meaninglessness of it all. . . . They are all wagers on value; and value is a wager on the transcendent and universal." Ward, "How Literature Resists Secularity," 77.

41. Krasnik, "'It No Longer Feels a Great Injustice That I Have to Die.'"

THREE.   Beyond the Brain

1. Francine Prose explained why she wanted to interview Davis: "I was glad for a chance to talk to her about her new story collection, *Almost No Memory*, and for an opportunity to ask questions I'd wondered about for years — to try and find out what makes her writing so original, so unique, so thrillingly

peculiar." Prose, "Lydia Davis." Ben Marcus caused a bit of a stir with that last designation. See Marcus, "Analyze This." Dan Chiasson wrote that her stories "belong to the class 'fiction' but also to the larger class made up of all things isolated in time or space: specimen creatures in jars, radar blips that promise interstellar life, Beckett's characters on a desolated stage, or John Cage's notes dispersed across silence." Chiasson, "Horse Sense & Heartache."

2. Davis said, "Sometimes I think what interests me most is the human mind . . . and thinking more than anything else. An experience was just an excuse to see how the mind works." Knight, "An Interview with Lydia Davis," 530.

3. And Samuel Beckett, whose novel *The Unnamable* she found on her English professor father's desk when she was thirteen. "It made a very strong impression because it was so different from anything I had read. I opened this book and it said on the first page, 'I'm lying here. I've dropped my pencil.'" Prose, "Lydia Davis."

4. Lehrer, *Proust Was a Neuroscientist*; Wolf, *Proust and the Squid*.

5. Damasio, *Self Comes to Mind*, 79; original emphasis. For insight into how this challenges (for example) Lockean views of the self and language, see Taylor, *The Language Animal*.

6. Jacques Derrida famously wrote, "il n'y a pas de hors-texte": there is no outside-text. We now know "il n'y a pas du hors-chair": there is no outside-flesh. Many thanks to the anonymous reviewer who pointed out the distinction between *corpse* (my original term) and *chair* in French.

7. Lakoff and Johnson, *Metaphors We Live By*. See also Johnson, *The Body in the Mind*.

8. Turner, *The Literary Mind*, 29.

9. Damasio, *Self Comes to Mind*, 117.

10. The *Poetics* is committed to a mind-body-emotion connection as the basis of how fiction operates. As Paul Armstrong points out, "Aristotle may have been wrong about the purging effects of catharsis, but he was right about the embodiment of aesthetic emotions." Armstrong, *How Literature Plays with the Brain*, 125.

11. Davis, *Varieties of Disturbance*. Subsequent references to this work are cited parenthetically in the text.

12. Armstrong, *How Literature Plays with the Brain*. Armstrong argues that neuroscience requires phenomenology as much as phenomenology requires neuroscience. To ignore this fact is to be limited by metaphysical naturalism, which can tell only one side of the story.

13. This balance between the desire for both novelty and constancy has been observed by the neuroscientist Ian McGilchrist as well, with the added observation that it is the left hemisphere of the brain that primarily is drawn to discrete details that it considers central and the right hemisphere that concerns itself with seeing how those parts fit into the whole. McGilchrist, *The Master and His Emissary*.

14. Davis, *Can't and Won't*, 32. Further references are cited parenthetically in the text as *Can't*.

15. For two different stories of the origin of the novel, see McKeon, *The Origins of the English Novel, 1600–1740*; Watt, *The Rise of the Novel*.

16. Lodge, *Consciousness and the Novel*, 42.

17. When they began their research, David Comer Kidd and Emanuele Castano surmised, correctly (following the lead of Jerome Bruner), that "whereas many of our mundane social experiences may be scripted by convention and informed by stereotypes, those presented in literary fiction often disrupt our expectations. Readers of literary fiction must draw on more flexible interpretive resources to infer the feelings and thoughts of characters. That is, they must engage ToM processes. Contrary to literary fiction, popular fiction, which is more readerly, tends to portray the world and characters as internally consistent and predictable. Therefore, it may reaffirm readers' expectations and so not promote ToM." Kidd and Castano, "Reading Literary Fiction Improves Theory of Mind," 378.

18. "Can cognitive science tell us why we are afraid of *Mrs. Dalloway*?," Zunshine's subheading asks. Yes, because the book requires us to read minds on multiple levels in order to make sense of it. Zunshine, *Why We Read Fiction*, 27. As one of my anonymous reviewers aptly pointed out, Zunshine's work does little to explain, from an evolutionary perspective, the sheer gratuitousness of ToM in *Mrs. Dalloway*.

19. The term "transdisciplinary" is Herman's. It expresses his desire for researchers from three cultures, the natural sciences, the social sciences, and the humanities, to "converge on the mind-narrative nexus . . . in a way that fosters genuine dialogue and exchange" rather than subordinate one to the others. Herman, *Storytelling and the Sciences of Mind*. Consilience as promoted by sociobiology and literary Darwinism would prevent that goal.

20. Herman, *Storytelling and the Sciences of Mind*, 23. It is interesting that Herman draws on Nancy Baker's research that highlights the robust first-person perspective I have been referring to in this book.

21. As far as I can tell, Herman is using the word *intentionality* to refer to authorial intention, not in its larger phenomenological definition. I address that kind of intentionality in chapter 4.

22. Herman spells out the sources and manifestations of this anti-intentionalism bias in narrative study. Herman, *Storytelling and the Sciences of Mind*, 37.

23. Yes, fictional, but as I have repeatedly argued, narration makes no sense if the narrator does not act in a way consistent with real persons. In response to a question about her narrators being autistic, Davis replied that they were not. In "We Miss You," she notes that "the almost maniacally single-minded narrator (presumably a sociologist) focuses unwaveringly on a detailed analysis of the children's letters without betraying any emotional reactions of her own. And yet there are hints that she is fighting to maintain her own neutrality and her 'scientific' detachment. Emotion is central to the story, as it is to most of the stories." Manguso, "Interview with Lydia Davis."

24. Paul Zak, a neuroscientist known for his work on the neurochemical oxytocin, has researched the powerful effect that fictional narrative has on our real-world actions. His research consistently revealed that the more readers are concerned for characters, the more powerful the outcome for future behavior,

such as donating money to related causes. "If you pay attention to the story and become emotionally engaged with the stories characters, then it is as if you have been transported into the stories world." Zak, "Why Inspiring Stories Make Us React," 5–6.

25. They appear to be banal, but most certainly are not. In fact, Robbin writes that "when Lydia Davis is writing, she makes everyone else look like they're transcribing spam. 'They are motionless until they move again,' she writes of the cows. To whom else, besides perhaps Wallace Stevens, would it occur to make such an observation?" Robbins, "Review: 'Can't and Won't' by Lydia Davis."

26. It is an ontological reality that is in a dispositional category related to human persons, not a thing like an apple is a thing. The upshot of this is the metaphysical conclusion that "persons are fundamentally different kinds of beings from anything else in the natural world." Baker, *Naturalism and the First-Person Perspective*, 155.

27. Ibid., 50.

28. In fact, Searle reports at the end of *The Mystery of Consciousness* that he has gotten even more pushback against his ideas from adherents of computational theories of mind than from religious believers in the soul: "Some computationalists invest an almost religious intensity into their faith that our deepest problems about the mind will have a computational solution. Many people apparently believe that somehow or other, unless we are proven to be computers, something terribly important will be lost." He speculates that the reasons for this involve a "certain technological will to power" (189–90).

29. Searle explains that "Dennett argues that there is no such thing as conscious life, for us, for animals, for zombies, or for anything else; there is only complex zombiehood." Searle, *The Mystery of Consciousness*, 107.

30. Ibid., 212.

31. Siegel, *Pocket Guide to Interpersonal Neurobiology*, 9–2.

32. This step to the idea of intersubjectivity as constitutive of the self is, of course, a big one for anyone to take. While I discussed this idea from a theological perspective in chapter 1, it is useful here to notice how far neuroscience has progressed in confirming it. The discovery of mirror neurons can be seen as taking a step in that direction. In 1999 experiments done with monkeys revealed that the same neurons fired in the brains of the monkeys who watched other monkeys performing actions (such as picking up a piece of fruit) as the neurons of the monkeys performing the actions themselves. Acharya and Shukla, "Mirror Neurons." Enough research on mirror neurons in human beings has transpired since then to permit scholars to conclude that they are "the glue that binds primary intersubjectivity." Armstrong, *How Literature Plays with the Brain*, 139. While the existence of mirror neurons does not prove that intersubjectivity produces our sense of self, it certainly moves in that direction. At the very least, it is enough to make us understand that reading stories depends on our exercising a kind of nonidentical doubling activity at the deepest levels of conscious and nonconscious cognition.

33. Bakhtin, *Speech Genres and Other Late Essays*, 68. As we saw in chapter 1, this definition of *utterance* also concurs with Derek Attridge's insistence

on the literary text as a singular event, not a thing. My response to the singularity of the text "will also be an unpredictable, singular affirmation of the singular event of the work's otherness as it impinges on me, here and now, in this event of reading." Attridge, *The Singularity of Literature*, 128.

34. The reader should note that while I consider phenomenology inherently resistant to scientific naturalism, some efforts have been made within phenomenology to account for it. See Carel and Meacham, *Phenomenology and Naturalism*. One of the best articulations of the resistant position that I have read is from Jean-Luc Marion, who argues that when phenomena are considered in their essential givenness they are unintelligible as brute facts or mere objects. See Marion, *Being Given*, bk. 1.

35. Regina Dürig draws attention to the inherently personal nature of storytelling by focusing on a real-life event that both Lydia Davis and her then-partner, Paul Auster, related in different stories. The couple had been completely out of money and managed to burn the only food they had left in the house: the onion pie they were making for dinner. Dürig, "The Onion Pie as Souvenir."

36. There is over a century of stucturalist and poststructuralist theory loaded in these terms. By "sign," I am referring to the Saussurean definition of the combination of *signifier* (the word/sound "stop") and *signified* (the concept of the imperative, stop!). Saussure argued that signs had no positive content but could only be known because of their difference from other signs. Saussure, *Course in General Linguistics*.

37. Baker, *Naturalism and the First-Person Perspective*, 155.

38. Bakhtin, *Speech Genres and Other Late Essays*, 126–27.

39. de Lubac, *The Discovery of God*, 35.

40. Ibid., 99. De Lubac is quoting Martin Buber.

41. Ibid., 36.

42. David Lodge gives the fiction of Alain Robbe-Grillet as an example of this type. Because he was an uncompromising materialist and atheist, Robbe-Grillet was "calling for a literature without qualia." Lodge argues that the fiction he wrote in accordance with this idea "seems to me almost unendurably tedious, except when the human emotions he tried to expunge manage to insinuate themselves back into the text." Lodge, *Consciousness and the Novel*, 79. Once again, the exception of Robbe-Grillet only proves the rule.

43. Prose, "Lydia Davis."

44. As Andrew Newberg explains, the important thing is allowing for the possibility that our intuition that we are connected to a larger consciousness is true. Newberg, *Principles of Neurotheology*, 62.

FOUR.   Beyond Evolution

1. Boyd, *On the Origin of Stories*, 81.

2. Among books written within literary studies with an interest in cognitive science, Paul Armstrong's is a notable exception for its resistance to foreclosing metaphysical questions. Armstrong, *How Literature Plays with the Brain*.

3. Boyd, *On the Origin of Stories*, 149.

4. Ibid., 202.

5. As I mentioned earlier, there have been some efforts to naturalize phenomenology. See Carel and Meacham, *Phenomenology and Naturalism*.

6. O'Connor, *Collected Works*, 59. Subsequent quotations are cited parenthetically in the text.

7. Allen, "The Cage of Matter," 257.

8. I am addressing the animal/human difference in this chapter only in regard to cognition and acts of recognition. But Aaron Hillyer draws on Agamben's theories to make a compelling case for *Wise Blood* as illustrative of a mid-century political battle over who has the right to define what is human and what is animal. That is, the story reveals how advanced industrial societies employ the dichotomous categories of human and animal in order to effectively "other" whole groups of people that the authorities at large would like to abuse or exterminate. See Hillyer, "Becoming Human, Becoming Animal."

9. Scientists are discovering that the lion's share (as it were) of human activity takes place at this level, often called nonconscious cognition. See Hayles, "Cognition Everywhere."

10. Johnson, *The Meaning of the Body*, 34.

11. Ibid., 40.

12. This is not an argument for or against evolution but a statement about on-the-ground realities of the native capacities and behaviors of the different species of which we are currently aware. Without human intervention, explains Derek Bickerton, animals do not learn or use language. Apes in and out of captivity "have been studied by many acute and highly motivated observers for nearly half a century. The behaviors of these species have been described and discussed and analyzed over and over again. Yet not one researcher has ever come up with any behavior that seemed remotely languagelike. And with every year that passes, the likelihood that one ever will gets smaller and smaller." Bickerton, *Adam's Tongue*, 83.

13. Needless to say, it is impossible to summarize Bickerton's argument about chimps' linguistic capacities and abilities in one paragraph. He explains that the chimps' brains had to be rewired by repeated efforts on the part of trainers, and even then, the symbols employed lacked the structure inherent to human language, even ASL. He writes, "Two things only could have triggered the growth of the neural network that made it possible to connect arbitrary signals with things in the outside world. One of them, the one that worked for apes, was a deliberate act of intervention by another species: us. The other, the one that worked for our remote ancestors, was factor X—the factor this book is looking for." Bickerton, *Adam's Tongue*, 83. It is worth noting that Bickerton, a scientific naturalist, has de facto excluded that factor X can have been caused by anything other than early humans' environment and their responses to their environment. This de facto exclusion of phenomenological and theological resources and frameworks is what I am challenging in this book.

14. For a useful breakdown of these studies and the implications, see Taylor, *The Language Animal*, ch. 2.

15. With regard to nonlinguistic artistic activity, this is somewhat more debatable; Brian Boyd sees the playful actions of dolphins (blowing bubbles with

design, "air art") as approximating human art. Boyd, *On the Origin of Stories*, 3–4. But no dolphins, as far as we know, tell stories.

16. According to Bickerton, the most promising current theory is "niche construction theory," which argues that individual behavior plays a bigger role in the eventual development of abilities within species than most evolutionary accounts acknowledge. Bickerton, *Adam's Tongue*, ch. 5.

17. Equally important is what the differences don't mean. To say that humans are fundamentally different from animals need not open the door to animal abuse or other insults to creation. Furthermore, as Robert Spaemann explains, arguments for the dignity of each human person (notably, the idea that one cannot be sacrificed for the interest of many, as in utilitarian ethics) must not be derived from the claim that humans are more valuable than other animal species. They "can only be derived from a claim of incommensurable value— incommensurable even with the dignity of other human beings. That is why we prefer to speak of human 'dignity' (*Würde*) rather than human 'value' (*Wert*)." Spaemann, *Persons*, 185.

18. For a thorough explanation of the difference between signal systems, protolanguage, and language, see Bickerton, *Adam's Tongue*, ch. 1.

19. Taylor, *The Language Animal*, 23.

20. That is, if the possibility were not foreclosed by metaphysical naturalism at the outset of inquiry into how language originated. This is why Bickerton insists that language is uniquely embedded in human biology, but "no serious scholar nowadays doubts that language is, at bottom, biological rather than cultural, and therefore was not created, but somehow evolved." Bickerton, *Adam's Tongue*, 92. I guess this means that Charles Taylor, for example, is not a serious scholar?

21. Taylor, *The Language Animal*, 28.

22. Sokolowski, *Phenomenology of the Human Person*, 56.

23. Ibid., 66, 69.

24. "On the contrary, showing something means that the one to whom something is shown sees it correctly for himself. It is in this sense that imitation is a showing. For imitation enables us to see more than so called reality. What is shown is, so to speak, elicited from the flux of manifold reality." Gadamer, *The Relevance of the Beautiful and Other Essays*, 128–29.

25. Boyd, *On the Origin of Stories*, 72.

26. In a letter, O'Connor explained, "That Haze rejects that mummy suggests everything. What he has been looking for with body and soul throughout the book is suddenly presented to him and he sees it has to be rejected, he sees it ain't really what he's looking for. I don't regard it in any abstracted sense at all." O'Connor, *The Habit of Being*, 404.

27. Ellen Dissanayake argues that the arts, like ritual, were devised by humans from a universal need to separate the ordinary from the extraordinary or "make special." Although this explanation is viable and far superior to many other evolutionary-based guesses of what behaviors comprise the core of the arts, her rhetorical move is familiar: "At some point in their evolution, humans began deliberately to set out to *make things special* or extra-ordinary, perhaps

for the purpose of influencing the outcome of important events that were perceived as uncertain and troubling, requiring action beyond simple fight or flight, approach or avoidance." Dissanayake, *Homo Aestheticus*, 51. To argue that "at some point" this just happened is no more a leap of faith than to argue that humans have recognized or had revealed to them that "this world is not conclusion" and their place in it is unique.

28. Balthasar, *The Glory of the Lord*, 1:237; original emphasis.

29. Ibid.

30. This is why de Lubac insisted that our first affirmation of God does not depend on reason in developing human beings. It is something we know viscerally first. "The affirmation of God rises up from the very roots of being and thought, before all conscious acts, before the formation of concepts, conferring upon consciousness its guarantee and upon the concept its universal validity." De Lubac, *The Discovery of God*, 105.

31. Romans 1:20, ESV.

32. While I don't want to disrupt the flow of my argument, I think it is important to explain the exact point of departure between my argument here and that of Mark Johnson in his book *The Meaning of the Body*, which I admire. Johnson fights dualism throughout the book but doesn't recognize how his metaphysical naturalism leads him to commit a similar error. At the end of his book in a section called "Embodied Spirituality" he argues that we must strive for a kind of transcendence that recognizes "the inescapability of human finitude and is compatible with the embodiment of meaning, mind, and personal identity." But to do so he creates a false dichotomy between that kind of transcendence, which he calls "horizontal," and what he takes to be all other versions, which he calls "vertical." "Love is a commitment to the well-being of others in a way that takes you at least partly beyond your ego-centered needs and desires and opens up your potential to respect and care for others and for your world. None of this is grounded in the infinite, but rather in the creative possibilities of finite human experience." Johnson, *The Meaning of the Body*, 281–82. Johnson's metaphysical naturalism leads him to a dualism that forecloses the possibility of the infinite that becomes embodied in the finite in the incarnation of Christ. For a detailed story of a transcendence that recognizes human finitude but does not foreclose God's existence, see Zimmermann, *Incarnational Humanism*.

33. Balthasar, *The Glory of the Lord*, 1:511. I'm indebted to an anonymous reviewer who pointed out that when it comes to experience, Balthasar, in contrast to Karl Rahner (and Friedrich Schleiermacher before him), favors the German concept *Erfahrung* over *Erlebnis*. O'Connor gave Haze the new jesus precisely because he would have preferred a purely personal and subjective experience over a revealed and pointedly objective one.

FIVE.   Beyond the Postsecular

1. For an excellent overview of the complex topography of postsecular scholarship in literary studies, see Corrigan, "The Postsecular and Literature."

"By far the most agreed upon aspect of the postsecular is that, in some way or other, it includes both the secular and the religious. But scholars differ on how the two do or should relate to each, and on whether they remain distinct."

2. Fessenden, *Culture and Redemption*. Roger Lundin argues that Fessenden simplifies religious motives because the goal of the book "is not to laud the liberty of secular experience but to expose the poverty, even the venality, of secular Protestantism, which has sold its ethical soul for the sake of its subtly concealed cultural control." Lundin, "Review of *Culture and Redemption*," 106.

3. In his review of the book, Timothy Aubry writes that "McClure is so intent on establishing the appeal of the postsecular by distinguishing it from traditional, dogmatic, fundamentalist religious practices and beliefs that his central concept at times runs the risk of losing its positive content, becoming merely a container for prevailing academic values with a vaguely spiritual inflection" (492). He continues, "The absurdity of religious orthodoxy is assumed rather than argued in his book, which is unsurprising given his audience, but this stance is somewhat ironic in light of his reflexive embrace of certain academic orthodoxies whose axiomatic status a study of postsecular thought might be a good place to question or at least rethink" (493). Aubry, "*Partial Faiths*."

4. McClure, *Partial Faiths*, 14. Yes, it certainly does resemble Hazel Motes's Church Without Christ.

5. Ibid.

6. Ibid., 128.

7. Hungerford, *Postmodern Belief*, 105. For Hungerford, this authority is necessarily at the vampiric expense of biblical authority, for the effort is to make the literary text a substitute for scripture.

8. Morrison, *Beloved*, 1. Subsequent citations appear parenthetically in the text.

9. Morrison and Taylor-Guthrie, *Conversations with Toni Morrison*, 226.

10. Morrison found a literal ghost no more incredible than the political realities illustrated in her novel: "The fully realized presence of the haunting is both a major incumbent of the narrative and sleight of hand. One of its purposes is to keep the reader preoccupied with the nature of the incredible spirit world while being supplied a controlled diet of the incredible political world." Morrison, "Unspeakable Things, Unspoken," in Solomon, *Critical Essays on Toni Morrison's "Beloved,"* 92.

11. Trudier Harris-Lopez begins with this observation and discusses the implications of gendering the demonic as female. Harris, *Fiction and Folklore*, 151–64.

12. Grotesques "body forth the threatedness of human existence, whether in terms of moral temptation, spiritual failure, or physical catastrophe. Encroaching evil, natural or human, is their recurring theme." Hazelton, "The Grotesque, Theologically Considered," 78.

13. Ibid.

14. Susan Corey argues that *Beloved* embraces both a positive and a negative grotesque, in that "the grotesque not only reveals the horror of slavery, but it also sets forth a vision of regeneration and healing." Corey, "Toward the Limits of Mystery," 33.

15. Gurleen Grewel argues that "in a way it is important that Beloved remain somewhat inaccessible and mysterious so as to be a suggestive symbol of the unconscious, of desire, of the past, of memory—for none of these is fully graspable by the conscious mind." Grewal, *Circles of Sorrow, Lines of Struggle*, 116.

16. Morrison and Taylor-Guthrie, *Conversations with Toni Morrison*, 85.

17. Ibid., 116.

18. Solomon, *Critical Essays on Toni Morrison's "Beloved,"* 39–42.

19. Kierkegaard, *The Sickness unto Death*, 50.

20. Ibid., 48.

21. Augustine contrasts the devil, who is the mediator of death, with Christ, who is the mediator of life. St. Augustine, *The Trinity*, 162.

22. Corey, "Toward the Limits of Mystery," 38.

23. Bakhtin, *Rabelais and His World*, 21.

24. Girard, *I See Satan Fall Like Lightning*, 32–46.

25. Ibid., 45.

26. Griesinger, "Why Baby Suggs, Holy, Quit Preaching the Word," 694; original emphasis.

27. Morrison and Taylor-Guthrie, *Conversations with Toni Morrison*, 147.

28. Harpham, *On the Grotesque*, 54–55.

29. Harris, *Fiction and Folklore*, 160. Caroline Rody pays attention to the implications of gender in her reading of this section, arguing that Morrison "conflates the problematics of time, loss, and representation with a drama of inconsumable female desire. Calling the past 'Beloved' and remembering it in a female body, the text gives one name to the loss of history and buried female desire, and it stages the simultaneous resurrection of both." Rody, "Toni Morrison's *Beloved*," 102.

30. Deborah Ayer Sitter argues that Morrison "shows how every natural instinct and emotion is in some way twisted or stunted by the experience of living in a culture that measures individual worth by resale value and the ability to reproduce oneself without cost." Sitter, "The Making of a Man," 190.

31. Girard, *Deceit, Desire, and the Novel*.

32. Morrison and Taylor-Guthrie, *Conversations with Toni Morrison*, 162.

33. Vernant, "Before Sexuality," 470.

34. Amy B. Brown argues that Morrison's novel *Song of Solomon* draws on the biblical book to revise the theme of love therein and therefore "indicates the productivity of the hermeneutics of suspicion in Morrison's reading of the Song of Songs." Brown, *Rewriting the Word*, 148. I think that Morrison is equally suspicious in *Beloved* that the West has overvalued erotic desire and thus perverted the concept of love as charity.

35. Eusebio L. Rodrigues argues that the structure of the novel is musical, not aural, and that these central sections are composed of a trio of voices singing a liturgical dirge. Rodrigues, "The Telling of *Beloved*," 74.

36. Morrison and Taylor-Guthrie, *Conversations with Toni Morrison*, 249; original emphasis.

37. As Jürgen Moltmann argues, the incarnation of the Son is a move toward an ever-widening circle of love. "In the incarnation of the Son *the Trinity* throws itself open, as it were. The Father of the Son becomes the Father of the

new, free and united human race." Moltmann, *The Trinity and the Kingdom*, 121–22.

38. Augustine, *The Trinity*, 253.

39. Ibid., 219–20.

40. Vernant, "Before Sexuality," 477.

41. David Lawrence argues that the "fusion of identity expressed in this refrain can only be destructive, as Sethe and Denver lose themselves in the overpowering 'mine' asserted by Beloved. In the end, their 'conversation' is a monologic discourse dictated by a fleshly ghost, a univocal tyranny silencing any attempt at dialogic communication." Lawrence, "Fleshly Ghosts and Ghostly Flesh," 53.

42. Much of the poetry of Czeslaw Milosz touches on this theme. For example:

. . .

And though the good is weak, beauty is very strong.
Nonbeing sprawls, everywhere it turns into ash whole expanses of being,
It masquerades in shapes and colors that imitate existence
And no one would know it, if they did not know that it was ugly.

. . .

From Milosz, "One More Day," in *New & Collected Poems, 1931–2001*, 418–19.

43. For Elizabeth Fox-Genovese's astute discussion of the implications of the repression of the difficult stories of slavery, see Bauerlein, *History and Women, Culture and Faith*, 174–93.

44. Zizioulas, *Being as Communion*, 17.

SIX.   Beyond Beauty

1. Hungerford, *Postmodern Belief*, 95.

2. Ibid., 137.

3. O'Connor, *Mystery and Manners*. O'Connor writes that "from the standpoint of the writer, it is safe to say that while the South is hardly Christ-centered, it is most certainly Christ-haunted. The Southerner, who isn't convinced of it, is very much afraid that he may have been formed in the image and likeness of God. Ghosts can be very fierce and instructive. They cast strange shadows, particularly in our literature" (44–45).

4. Taylor, *A Secular Age*, 539–93.

5. Steiner, *Grammars of Creation*, 45.

6. McCarthy, *The Road*, 15. Subsequent citations of this novel are given parenthetically in the text.

7. In Vanhoozer et al., *Dictionary for Theological Interpretation of the Bible*, 386.

8. Crane, *The Red Badge of Courage and Other Stories*, 139.

9. Wood, *The Fun Stuff*, 64.

10. Balthasar, *The Glory of the Lord*, vol. 1. The non-Platonic part is important because the incarnation of Christ moves the issue from the abstract and

universal to the concrete and particular. Beauty is not a Platonic universal for Balthasar.

11. Ibid., 18.

12. Ibid., 19; original emphasis.

13. Ibid., 21.

14. Ibid., 21–22; my emphasis.

15. McCarthy, *The Crossing*, 158.

16. As I mentioned in chapter 1, Balthasar's argument is very similar to that made by Bakhtin, who compares the author's consciousness to God's only in that it reveals that aesthetic vision is something that by definition a person cannot have of one's self. Bakhtin, *Art and Answerability*.

17. Lydia Cooper productively focuses on the father's own view of story-telling as a sacramental rite his son needs. His journey is "a moral quest to become a father, but the fathering of a human child is merged with the metaphoric journey toward authorship. *The Road* in particular emphasizes the creative force of language as a prophetic 'fathering' of humanity." Cooper, *No More Heroes*, 139. She also correctly identifies that the question at the center of this text and many of McCarthy's other novels is theological: "The boy is either a form drenched in sacramental meaning, or 'God never spoke' and the form is meaningless" (153–54).

18. Zimmermann, "'Quo Vadis'?," 515.

19. Maritain, in D'Souza and Seiling, *Being in the World*, 25.

20. Gabriel Marcel gives the example of a sleeping child as one that uniquely stirs us to recognize the mystery of presence in human beings. He argues that "we might say that it is just because this being is completely unprotected, that it is utterly at our mercy, that it is also invulnerable or sacred. And there can be no doubt at all that the strongest and most irrefutable mark of sheer barbarism that we could imagine would consist in the refusal to recognize this mysterious invulnerability." Marcel, *The Mystery of Being*, 1:216–17.

21. Whatever delight he may find in depicting corruption, McCarthy's conception of evil in this novel is primarily Augustinian. Evil is the absence of good. There is no point in *The Road* where the reader is led to celebrate or glory in evil, though we are led to contemplate the possible dissolving of good, the uncreation of creation as humankind descends into the worst version of itself. "'Goodness,'" writes Lydia Cooper, "may have all the concrete substance of gossamer, but its role in this, the postapocalyptic universe, is foregrounded in a way that is perhaps unique in McCarthy's corpus." Cooper, *No More Heroes*, 135.

22. McFadyen, *The Call to Personhood*, 32.

23. Mounier, *Personalism*, 23.

24. Quoted in Laird, *Into the Silent Land*, 37.

25. Scruton, *Beauty*, 13.

26. Hungerford, *Postmodern Belief*, 135–36. Ashley Kunsa offers a more compelling interpretation of passages like these by insisting that McCarthy refuses the postmodern condition: "McCarthy searches for the essential elements of story—character, meaningful action, etc.—that hold narration together when artifice, self-consciousness and irony are burned away." Kunsa, "Maps of the World in Its Becoming," 68.

SEVEN.   Beyond the Visible

1. Thomas Aquinas argued in his *Summa* that to love a person means to wish that person good. Aquinas, *Summa Theologica* 1.20.1.

2. Spaemann, *Love and the Dignity of Human Life*, 19.

3. Ibid., 6.

4. Spaemann, *Persons*, 185.

5. Ibid. It is important to note that Spaemann's position on the incommensurable value of human beings does not require speciesism. A person's dignity is an inherent property of being a person, not necessarily a claim that humans are superior to animals. The artists at Chauvet recognized the beauty and dignity of the animals all around them.

6. Spaemann, *Love and the Dignity of Human Life*, 17. This glow might also be what Immanuel Levinas notes about Heidegger's view of art: "Being as a whole—signification—glows in the works of poets and artists." Levinas, *Humanism of the Other*, 18.

7. Unsurprisingly, no stable definition exists for this elastic genre. Scott McCloud, who defines comics as sequential art, is cited most frequently. McCloud, *Understanding Comics*. I favor Thierry Groensteen's focus on "iconic solidarity" as the defining feature of this unique art form, though of course this definition has its limits also. See Groensteen, "The Impossible Definition," in Heer and Worcester, *A Comics Studies Reader*, 124–31.

8. Madden, *99 Ways to Tell a Story*.

9. Russian formalism advanced this theory of literature. See Culler, *Literary Theory*. The graphic form has special power to break into different audiences with powerful challenges to our stereotypes, even when those stereotypes seem to be reinforced in the drawings themselves. Art Spiegelman's breakthrough classic, *Maus*, depicted Nazis as cats, Jews as mice, and Poles as pigs. Most critics agree that the stereotyped images jar readers into seeing how much we stereotype others, rather than the reverse.

10. Clowes, *Wilson*. Subsequent citations of this novel are given parenthetically in the text.

11. The fact that this shifting view of Wilson cannot be captured in a film might be one of the reasons why the 2017 film *Wilson*, starring Woody Harrelson, did not receive great reviews.

12. Boxall, *The Value of the Novel*.

13. Chute, *Graphic Women*, 182–83. Chute argues that Alison Bechdel's *Fun Home* was pivotal in the development of this form related to issues of embodiment.

14. The term "iconic solidarity" comes from Thierry Groensteen, "The Impossible Definition," in Heer and Worcester, *A Comics Studies Reader*, 124–31.

15. McCloud, *Understanding Comics*, 44.

16. Emmanuel Mounier explains that "the indissoluble union of the soul and the body is the pivot of Christian thinking." Anyone who claims Christianity and speaks with contempt for the body, he argues, speaks under "false Christian credentials." Mounier, *Personalism*, 4.

17. Ibid., xx.

18. Ibid., 41.

19. Bakhtin, *Toward a Philosophy of the Act*, 62.

20. This is also why I agree with Scott McCloud that the medium of comics bears tremendous potential to expand our vision of those different from us. It can more effectively do so if the industry diversifies. McCloud, *Reinventing Comics*. The success of Marjorie Satrapi's *Persopolis* (published after McCloud's somewhat brooding manifesto) is a good indication that the market can bear the salutary push. Satrapi, *Persepolis*.

21. McCarthy, *Child of God*, 4.

22. "By giving itself and showing itself, fatherhood on principle gives and manifests more than itself; the event of its arrival in the visible thus provokes a phenomenal event that is in principle endless. Nowhere else does the character of being given (*Gegebenheit*)– in other words, the character of appearing in the mode of the given, which would almost deserve the neologism given-ness [*donnéité*]—announce itself as clearly as here, thus conferring on fatherhood an exceptional phenomenological privilege." Marion, *Negative Certainties*, 100.

23. Spaemann writes, "Because love aims at the person, it can let go of the 'that is just how you are,' and allow the other to distance himself from himself and have a new beginning." Spaemann, *Love and the Dignity of Human Life*, 16–17. Is this not what the genre of the novel provides us the ability to do with our own lives?

24. Marcel, *Mystery of Being*, 2:62.

25. Love for being in the world is defined by an "active refusal to treat itself as subjective, and it is in this refusal that it cannot be separated from faith; in fact it is faith." Ibid., 62.

26. McGuire, *Here*. The book does not have page numbers.

27. The website tells us, "Completed in 1764, Proprietary House has served as a residence to New Jersey's last Royal Governor, a stylish hotel, a private mansion, a retirement home, a boarding house, and now a museum. A true survivor, this building has seen war and peace, fire and storms, neglect and restoration, to stand as a witness to 250 years of American history." www.theproprietary house.org.

28. McGuire told one interviewer, "The choking scene did happen. To a cousin of mine. Completely ridiculous. Someone is telling a joke about dying, and one of the ones listening to it laughs so hard that he suffers a deadly heart attack." Amat, "An Interview with Richard McGuire."

29. As McGuire has noted in numerous interviews, "I had a motto: Make the big moments small, and the small moments big. I wanted it to be about undocumented moments, the forgotten little things." See, e.g., Schuessler, "'Here,' Richard McGuire's Book, an Exhibition at the Morgan."

30. Chris Ware, one of the most well known of all graphic novelists, saw in McGuire's original strip (published in 1989 in the magazine *Raw*) all of this potential. McGuire captured "something closer to real memory and experience than anything that had come before." Schuessler, "'Here,' Richard McGuire's Book, an Exhibition at the Morgan."

31. Bachelard, *The Poetics of Space*, xxxvi.

32. Ibid., 5.

33. Ibid., 6.

34. Ibid., 208.

35. The implications of this choice could inform its own essay. The importance of ideas of home to seventeenth-century Dutch painters, for example, cannot be overstated. See Rybczynski, *Home*.

36. Amat, "An Interview with Richard McGuire."

37. Bachelard, *The Poetics of Space*, 7.

38. This is not, of course, to say that all human beings are born into well-being inside of safe homes. Bachelard is making a metaphysical claim in opposition to existential philosophies of being.

39. Gravett, *Comics Art*, 68. I also like the way Matt Seneca puts it: "In *Here*, we are a particularly fascinating species of flourishing fauna, a force as elemental in our time as the sun or the ocean. We've never seemed so small or so big, so important or so meaningless. Neither have comics." Seneca, "Here | The Comics Journal."

40. de Lubac, *The Mystery of the Supernatural*, 77.

41. Cooke, "*Here* by Richard McGuire Review—an Exquisitely Drawn Ecological Warning."

42. Fr. John-Julian, *The Complete Julian of Norwich*, 77.

WORKS CITED

Acharya, Sourya, and Samarth Shukla. "Mirror Neurons: Enigma of the Metaphysical Modular Brain." *Journal of Natural Science, Biology, and Medicine* 3, no. 2 (2012): 118–24.

Allen, William Rodney. "The Cage of Matter: The World as Zoo in Flannery O'Connor's *Wise Blood*." *American Literature: A Journal of Literary History, Criticism, and Bibliography* 58, no. 2 (May 1986): 256–70.

Amat, Kiko. "An Interview with Richard McGuire: 'I Want All My Work to Be Fun and at the Same Time a Bit Avant-Garde.' By Kiko Amat." O Production Company, April 12, 2016. http://abcdefghijklmn-pqrstuvwxyz.com /en/an-interview-with-richard-mcguire-i-want-all-my-work-to-be-fun -and-at-the-same-time-bit-avant-garde/.

Aquinas, St. Thomas. *Summa Theologica*. https://dhspriory.org/thomas/summa /index.html.

Armstrong, Paul B. *How Literature Plays with the Brain: The Neuroscience of Reading and Art*. Baltimore, MD: Johns Hopkins University Press, 2014.

Attridge, Derek. *The Singularity of Literature*. Abingdon: Routledge, 2017.

Aubry, Timothy Richard. *"Partial Faiths*: Postsecular Fiction in the Age of Pynchon and Morrison (Review)." *Studies in the Novel* 41, no. 4 (2010): 492–94.

Augustine, Saint. *The Trinity*. Edited by John E. Rotelle, OSA. Hyde Park, NY: New City Press, 2012.

Bachelard, Gaston. *The Poetics of Space*. Translated by Maria Jolas. Foreword by John R. Stilgoe. Boston: Beacon Press, 1994.

Baker, Lynne Rudder. *Naturalism and the First-Person Perspective*. Oxford: Oxford University Press, 2013.

Bakhtin, M. M. *Art and Answerability: Early Philosophical Essays*. Translated by Kenneth Brostrom. Edited by Michael Holquist and Vadim Liapunov. Austin: University of Texas Press, 1990.

———. *The Dialogic Imagination: Four Essays*. Edited by Michael Holquist. Translated by Caryl Emerson. Reprint ed. Austin: University of Texas Press, 1982.

———. *Rabelais and His World*. Bloomington: Indiana University Press, 1984.

———. *Speech Genres and Other Late Essays*. Austin: University of Texas Press, 1986.

———. *Toward a Philosophy of the Act*. Austin: University of Texas Press, 1993.

Bal, Mieke. *Narratology: Introduction to the Theory of Narrative*. Toronto: University of Toronto Press, 2009.

Balthasar, Hans Urs von. *The Glory of the Lord: A Theological Aesthetics*. Vol. 1: *Seeing the Form*. Edited by John Kenneth Riches. San Francisco: Ignatius Press, 2009.

Barth, John. *Lost in the Funhouse: Fiction for Print, Tape, Live Voice*. Garden City, NY: Doubleday, 1968.

Barthes, Roland. *Image-Music-Text*. Translated by Stephen Heath. New York: Hill and Wang, 1978.

Bauerlein, Mark. *History and Women, Culture and Faith: Selected Writings of Elizabeth Fox-Genovese*. Vol. 2: *Ghosts and Memories: White and Black Southern Women's Lives and Writings*. Edited by Kibibi Mack-Shelton and Christina Bieber Lake. Columbia: University of South Carolina Press, 2011.

Benjamin, Walter. *Illuminations: Essays and Reflections*. Edited by Hannah Arendt. Translated by Harry Zohn. New York: Schocken Books, 1969.

Bickerton, Derek. *Adam's Tongue: How Humans Made Language, How Language Made Humans*. New York: Hill and Wang, 2009.

Blanchot, Maurice. *The Space of Literature*. Translated by Ann Smock. Lincoln: University of Nebraska Press, 1989.

Boxall, Peter. *The Value of the Novel*. New York: Cambridge University Press, 2015.

Boyd, Brian. *On the Origin of Stories: Evolution, Cognition, and Fiction*. Cambridge, MA: Belknap Press of Harvard University Press, 2009.

Brown, Amy Benson. *Rewriting the Word: American Women Writers and the Bible*. Westport, CT: Greenwood, 1999.

Carel, Havi, and Darian Meacham, eds. *Phenomenology and Naturalism: Examining the Relationship between Human Experience and Nature*. Cambridge: Cambridge University Press, 2013.

CBS News. "Philip Roth on Fame, Sex and God." October 2010. www.cbsnews.com/news/philip-roth-on-fame-sex-and-god/.

Chiasson, Dan. "Horse Sense & Heartache." *New York Review of Books*. April 29, 2010. Accessed June 7, 2017. www.nybooks.com/articles/2010/04/29/horse-sense-heartache/.

Chute, Hillary. *Graphic Women: Life Narrative and Contemporary Comics*. New York: Columbia University Press, 2010.

Cixous, Hélène, Sandra M. Gilbert, and Catherine Clément. *Newly Born Woman*. Translated by Betsy Wing. Minneapolis: University of Minnesota Press, 1986.

Clowes, Daniel. *Wilson*. Montreal: Drawn and Quarterly, 2010.

Cooke, Rachel. "*Here* by Richard McGuire Review—an Exquisitely Drawn Ecological Warning." *Guardian*, December 21, 2014, Books. www.theguardian.com/books/2014/dec/21/here-richard-mcguire-review-exquisitely-drawn-ecological-warning.

Cooper, Lydia R. *No More Heroes: Narrative Perspective and Morality in Cormac McCarthy.* Baton Rouge: Louisiana State University Press, 2011.

Corey, Susan. "Toward the Limits of Mystery: The Grotesque in Toni Morrison's *Beloved.*" In *The Aesthetics of Toni Morrison: Speaking the Unspeakable,* edited and introduction by Marc C. Conner, 31–48. Jackson: University Press of Mississippi, 2000.

Corrigan, Paul T. "The Postsecular and Literature." *Corrigan Literary Review* (blog), May 17, 2015. https://corriganliteraryreview.wordpress.com/2015/05/17/the-postsecular-and-literature/.

Crane, Stephen. *The Red Badge of Courage and Other Stories.* Oxford: Oxford University Press, 2008.

Culler, Jonathan. *Literary Theory: A Very Short Introduction.* Oxford: Oxford University Press, 2011.

Dadlez, E. M., and C. M. Haramia. "Fictional Objects, Future Objectives: Why Existence Matters Less Than You Think." *Philosophy and Literature* 39, no. 1A (September 2015): A1–A15.

Damasio, Antonio. *Self Comes to Mind: Constructing the Conscious Brain.* New York: Vintage, 2012.

Dames, Nicholas. "The New Fiction of Solitude." *Atlantic,* April 2016. www.theatlantic.com/magazine/archive/2016/04/the-new-fiction-of-solitude/471474/.

Davis, Lydia. *Can't and Won't: Stories.* New York: Picador, 2015.

——. *Varieties of Disturbance: Stories.* New York: Farrar, Straus and Giroux, 2007.

Degler, Carl N. *In Search of Human Nature: The Decline and Revival of Darwinism in American Social Thought.* New York: Oxford University Press, 1991.

de Lubac, Henri. *The Discovery of God.* Grand Rapids, MI: Eerdmans, 1996.

Dennett, Daniel Clement. *Breaking the Spell: Religion as a Natural Phenomenon.* New York: Viking, 2006.

——. "How to Protect Human Dignity from Science." In *Human Dignity and Bioethics,* edited by Edmund D. Pellegrino, Adam Schulman, and Thomas W. Merrill, 39–59. Notre Dame, IN: University of Notre Dame Press, 2009.

Dissanayake, Ellen. *Homo Aestheticus: Where Art Comes From and Why.* Seattle: University of Washington Press, 1995.

——. *What Is Art For?* Seattle: University of Washington Press, 1990.

Dreyfus, Hubert, and Sean Dorrance Kelly. *All Things Shining: Reading the Western Classics to Find Meaning in a Secular Age.* New York: Free Press, 2011.

D'Souza, Mario, CSB, and Jonathan R. Seiling, eds. *Being in the World: A Quotable Maritain Reader.* Notre Dame, IN: University of Notre Dame Press, 2014.

Duban, James. "From Negative Identity to Existential Nothingness: Philip Roth and the Younger Jewish Intellectuals." *Partial Answers: Journal of Literature and the History of Ideas* 13, no. 1 (January 2015): 43–55.

Dürig, Regina. "The Onion Pie as Souvenir: The In Between of Writing as a Space of Meeting the Other." *Technoetic Arts: A Journal of Speculative Research* 13, no. 3 (2015): 285–89.

Dutton, Denis. *The Art Instinct: Beauty, Pleasure, and Human Evolution.* New York: Bloomsbury Press, 2010.

Felch, Susan M., and Paul J. Contino. *Bakhtin and Religion: A Feeling for Faith.* Evanston, IL: Northwestern University Press, 2001.

Fessenden, Tracy. *Culture and Redemption: Religion, the Secular, and American Literature.* Reprint ed. Princeton, NJ: Princeton University Press, 2013.

Flood, Alison. "Philip Roth Insists 'I Have No Desire to Write Fiction.'" *Guardian*, February 4, 2014, sec. Books. www.theguardian.com/books /2014/ feb/04/philip-roth-no-desire-write-fiction-novelist.

Gadamer, Hans-Georg. *The Relevance of the Beautiful and Other Essays.* Edited by Robert Bernasconi. Translated by Nicholas Walker. Cambridge: Cambridge University Press, 1987.

Girard, René. *Deceit, Desire, and the Novel: Self and Other in Literary Structure.* Baltimore, MD: Johns Hopkins University Press, 1976.

———. *I See Satan Fall Like Lightning.* Maryknoll, NY: Orbis Books; Ottawa: Novalis; Leominster: Gracewing, 2001.

Gogol, Nikolaï. *Dead Souls: The Reavey Translation, Backgrounds and Sources, Essays in Criticism.* New York: W. W. Norton, 1985.

Gottschall, Jonathan. *Literature, Science, and a New Humanities.* New York: Palgrave Macmillan, 2008.

———. *The Storytelling Animal: How Stories Make Us Human.* Boston: Mariner Books, 2013.

Gravett, Paul. *Comics Art.* New Haven, CT: Yale University Press, 2014.

Grewal, Gurleen. *Circles of Sorrow, Lines of Struggle: The Novels of Toni Morrison.* Baton Rouge: Louisiana State University Press, 1998.

Griesinger, Emily. "Why Baby Suggs, Holy, Quit Preaching the Word: Redemption and Holiness in Toni Morrison's *Beloved.*" *Christianity and Literature* 50, no. 4 (Summer 2001): 689–702.

Guajardo, Charles. *The Dot and the Line: A Romance in Lower Mathematics.* n.d. www.youtube.com/watch?v=OmSbdvzbOzY.

Gunton, Colin E. *The One, the Three and the Many: God, Creation and the Culture of Modernity.* Cambridge: Cambridge University Press, 1993.

Harpham, Geoffrey Galt. *On the Grotesque: Strategies of Contradiction in Art and Literature.* Aurora, CO: Davies Group Publishers, 2006.

Harris, Trudier. *Fiction and Folklore: The Novels of Toni Morrison.* Knoxville: University of Tennessee Press, 1991.

Hart, David Bentley. *The Experience of God: Being, Consciousness, Bliss.* New Haven, CT: Yale University Press, 2014.

Hayes, Patrick. *Philip Roth: Fiction and Power.* New York: Oxford University Press, 2014.

Hayles, N. Katherine. "Cognition Everywhere: The Rise of the Cognitive Nonconscious and the Costs of Consciousness." *New Literary History: A Journal of Theory and Interpretation* 45, no. 2 (Spring 2014): 199–220.

———. *How We Became Posthuman: Virtual Bodies in Cybernetics, Literature, and Informatics*. Chicago: University of Chicago Press, 1999.

Hazelton, Roger. "The Grotesque, Theologically Considered." In *The Grotesque in Art and Literature: Theological Reflections*, edited by James Luther Adams and Wilson Yates, 75–81. Grand Rapids, MI: Eerdmans, 1997.

Heer, Jeet, and Kent Worcester, eds. *A Comics Studies Reader*. Jackson: University Press of Mississippi, 2009.

Herman, David. *The Cambridge Companion to Narrative*. Cambridge: Cambridge University Press, 2007.

———. *Storytelling and the Sciences of Mind*. Cambridge, MA: MIT Press, 2013.

Hillyer, Aaron. "Becoming Human, Becoming Animal: The Anthropological Machine at Work in *Wise Blood*." In *Wise Blood: A Re-Consideration*, edited by John J. Han, 119–40. Dialogue 13. Amsterdam: Rodopi, 2011.

Hungerford, Amy. *Postmodern Belief: American Literature and Religion since 1960*. Princeton, NJ: Princeton University Press, 2010.

Hutto, Daniel D., ed. *Narrative and Understanding Persons*. Cambridge: Cambridge University Press, 2007.

John-Julian, Father, OJN. *The Complete Julian of Norwich*. Paraclete Giants. Brewster, MA: Paraclete Press, 2009.

Johnson, Mark. *The Body in the Mind: The Bodily Basis of Meaning, Imagination, and Reason*. 1st ed. Chicago: University of Chicago Press, 1990.

———. *The Meaning of the Body: Aesthetics of Human Understanding*. Reprint ed. Chicago: University of Chicago Press, 2008.

Jokinen, Tom. "Last of the Great Male Narcissists?" *Hazlitt Magazine*. Accessed July 9, 2015. http://penguinrandomhouse.ca/hazlitt/feature/last-great-male-narcissists.

Juster, Norton. *The Dot and the Line: A Romance in Lower Mathematics*. New York: Chronicle Books, 2000.

Kearney, Richard. *On Stories*. London: Routledge, 2002.

Kidd, David Comer, and Emanuele Castano. "Reading Literary Fiction Improves Theory of Mind." *Science* 342, no. 6156 (October 18, 2013): 377–80.

Kierkegaard, Søren. *The Sickness unto Death: A Christian Psychological Exposition for Upbuilding and Awakening*. Edited by Alastair Hannay. New York: Penguin Classics, 1989.

Knapp, Kathy. *American Unexceptionalism: The Everyman and the Suburban Novel after 9/11*. Iowa City: University of Iowa Press, 2014.

Knapp, Steven, and Walter Benn Michaels. "Against Theory." *Critical Inquiry* 8, no. 4 (1982): 723–42.

Knight, Christopher J. "An Interview with Lydia Davis." *Contemporary Literature* 40, no. 4 (Winter 1999): 525–51.

Krasnik, Martin. "'It No Longer Feels a Great Injustice That I Have to Die.'" *Guardian*, December 14, 2005, sec. Books. www.theguardian.com/books/2005/dec/14/fiction.philiproth.

Kunsa, Ashley. "Maps of the World in Its Becoming: Post-Apocalyptic Naming in Cormac McCarthy's *The Road*." *Journal of Modern Literature* 33, no. 1 (2009): 57–74.

Laird, Martin. *Into the Silent Land: A Guide to the Christian Practice of Contemplation*. Oxford: Oxford University Press, 2006.

Lakoff, George, and Mark Johnson. *Metaphors We Live By*. Chicago: University of Chicago Press, 2003.

Lawrence, David. "Fleshly Ghosts and Ghostly Flesh: The Word and the Body in *Beloved*." In *Toni Morrison's Fiction: Contemporary Criticism*, edited by David L. Middleton, 231–46. New York: Garland, 1997.

Lehrer, Jonah. *Proust Was a Neuroscientist*. Boston: Houghton Mifflin Harcourt, 2007.

Levinas, Emmanuel. *Humanism of the Other*. Translated by Nidra Poller. Introduction by Richard A. Cohen. Reprint ed. Urbana: University of Illinois Press, 2005.

Lezard, Nicholas. "*Nemesis* by Philip Roth—Review." *Guardian*, September 27, 2011, Books. www.theguardian.com/books/2011/sep/27/nemesis-philip-roth-review.

Lodge, David. *Consciousness and the Novel: Connected Essays*. Cambridge, MA: Harvard University Press, 2004.

———. *The Mystery of the Supernatural*. New York: Crossroad, 1998.

Lundin, Roger. "Review of *Culture and Redemption: Religion, the Secular, and American Literature*, by Tracy Fessenden." *Religion & Literature* 40, no. 3 (2008): 105–9.

Madden, Matt. *99 Ways to Tell a Story: Exercises in Style*. New York: Chamberlain Bros., 2005.

Manguso, Sarah. "Interview with Lydia Davis." *Believer*, January 1, 2008. www.believermag.com/issues/200801/?read=interview_davis.

Marcel, Gabriel. *The Mystery of Being*. Vol. 1: *Reflection and Mystery*. Translated by René Hague. South Bend, IN: St. Augustine's Press, 2001.

———. *Mystery of Being*. Vol. 2: *Faith and Reality*. South Bend, IN: St. Augustine's Press, 2001.

Marcus, Ben. "Analyze This." *Bookforum*, May 2007. www.bookforum.com/inprint/014_01/172.

Marion, Jean-Luc. *Being Given: Toward a Phenomenology of Givenness*. Translated by Jeffrey L. Kosky. Stanford, CA: Stanford University Press, 2002.

———. *Negative Certainties*. Translated by Stephen E. Lewis. Chicago: University of Chicago Press, 2015.

Maritain, Jacques. *Person and the Common Good*. South Bend, IN: University of Notre Dame Press, 1973.

Masiero, Pia. *Philip Roth and the Zuckerman Books: The Making of a Storyworld*. Amherst, NY: Cambria Press, 2011.

McCarthy, Cormac. *Child of God*. New York: Vintage, 1993.

———. *The Crossing*. New York: Vintage, 1995.

———. *The Road*. New York: Alfred A. Knopf, 2006.

McCloud, Scott. *Reinventing Comics: The Evolution of an Art Form*. New York: William Morrow Paperbacks, 2000.

———. *Understanding Comics: The Invisible Art*. New York: William Morrow Paperbacks, 1994.

McClure, John A. *Partial Faiths: Postsecular Fiction in the Age of Pynchon and Morrison.* Athens: University of Georgia Press, 2007.

McFadyen, Alistair I. *The Call to Personhood: A Christian Theory of the Individual in Social Relationships.* Cambridge: Cambridge University Press, 1990.

McGilchrist, Iain. *The Master and His Emissary: The Divided Brain and the Making of the Western World.* New Haven, CT: Yale University Press, 2012.

McGuire, Richard. *Here.* New York: Pantheon, 2014.

McKeon, Michael. *The Origins of the English Novel, 1600–1740.* Baltimore, MD: Johns Hopkins University Press, 2002.

Milosz, Czeslaw. *New & Collected Poems, 1931–2001.* New York: Ecco Press, 2003.

Moltmann, Jürgen. *The Trinity and the Kingdom: The Doctrine of God.* Translated by Margaret Kohl. San Francisco: Harper & Row, 1981.

Morris, Desmond. "Can Jumbo Elephants Really Paint? Intrigued by Stories, Naturalist Desmond Morris Set out to Find the Truth." *Mail Online.* Accessed June 14, 2017. www.dailymail.co.uk/sciencetech/article-1151283/Can-jumbo-elephants-really-paint-Intrigued-stories-naturalist-Desmond-Morris-set-truth.html.

Morrison, Toni. *Beloved.* New York: Vintage, 2004.

Morrison, Toni, and Danille Kathleen Taylor-Guthrie. *Conversations with Toni Morrison.* Jackson: University Press of Mississippi, 1994.

Mounier, Emmanuel. *Personalism.* Notre Dame, IN: University of Notre Dame Press, 1989.

Nagel, Thomas. *Mind and Cosmos: Why the Materialist Neo-Darwinian Conception of Nature Is Almost Certainly False.* New York: Oxford University Press, 2012.

Naydan, Liliana M. *Rhetorics of Religion in American Fiction: Faith, Fundamentalism, and Fanaticism in the Age of Terror.* Lewisburg, PA: Bucknell University Press, 2016.

New York Times. "What Is the Best Work of American Fiction of the Last 25 Years?" Accessed June 9, 2017. www.nytimes.com/ref/books/fiction-25-years.html.

Newberg, Andrew B. *Principles of Neurotheology.* Farnham: Ashgate, 2010.

O'Connor, Flannery. *Collected Works.* New York: Library of America, 1988.

———. *The Habit of Being: Letters of Flannery O'Connor.* Edited by Sally Fitzgerald. New York: Farrar, Straus and Giroux, 1988.

———. *Mystery and Manners: Occasional Prose.* Selected and edited by Sally and Robert Fitzgerald. New York: Farrar, Straus and Giroux, 1969.

Parks, Tim. *Life and Work: Writers, Readers, and the Conversations between Them.* New Haven, CT: Yale University Press, 2016.

Pellegrino, Edmund D., Adam Schulman, and Thomas W. Merrill, eds. *Human Dignity and Bioethics.* Notre Dame, IN: University of Notre Dame Press, 2009.

Percy, Walker, and Patrick H. Samway. *Signposts in a Strange Land.* New York: Farrar, Straus and Giroux, 1991.

Phillips, Larry W., ed. *Ernest Hemingway on Writing*. New York: Touchstone, 1999.

Posnock, Ross. *Philip Roth's Rude Truth: The Art of Immaturity*. Princeton, NJ: Princeton University Press, 2006.

Prose, Francine. "Lydia Davis." *BOMB*, Summer 1997. http://bombmagazine .org/article/2086/lydia-davis.

Radner, Ephraim. *A Time to Keep: Theology, Mortality, and the Shape of a Human Life*. Waco, TX: Baylor University Press, 2017.

Ricoeur, Paul. *Oneself as Another*. Chicago: University of Chicago Press, 1992.

Robbins, Michael. "Review: 'Can't and Won't' by Lydia Davis." Accessed June 7, 2017. http://articles.chicagotribune.com/2014-04-04/features/chi-cant -and-wont-lydia-davis-20140404_1_printers-row-journal-new-story -digital-edition.

Roberts, Reverend Alexander, ed. *The Ante-Nicene Fathers: The Writings of the Fathers Down to A.D. 325*. Vol. 1: *The Apostolic Fathers with Justin Martyr and Irenaeus*. New York: Cosimo Classics, 2007.

Robinson, Marilynne. *Absence of Mind: The Dispelling of Inwardness from the Modern Myth of the Self*. New Haven, CT: Yale University Press, 2010.

———. *The Givenness of Things: Essays by Marilynne Robinson*. New York: Farrar, Straus and Giroux, 2015.

Rodrigues, Eusebio L. "The Telling of *Beloved*." In *Understanding Toni Morrison's "Beloved" and "Sula": Selected Essays and Criticisms of the Works by the Nobel Prize–Winning Author*, edited by Solomon O. Iyasere and Marla W. Iyasere, 61–82. Troy, NY: Whitston, 2000.

Rody, Caroline. "Toni Morrison's *Beloved*: History, 'Rememory,' and a 'Clamor for a Kiss.'" In *Understanding Toni Morrison's "Beloved" and "Sula": Selected Essays and Criticisms of the Works by the Nobel Prize–Winning Author*, edited by Solomon O. Iyasere and Marla W. Iyasere, 83–112. Troy, NY: Whitston, 2000.

Roth, Philip. *Conversations with Philip Roth*. Jackson: University Press of Mississippi, 1992.

———. *The Counterlife*. New York: Vintage, 1996.

———. *Everyman*. New York: Vintage, 2007.

———. *Reading Myself and Others*. New York: Vintage, 2001.

Ruse, Michael. *Darwinism as Religion: What Literature Tells Us about Evolution*. Oxford: Oxford University Press, 2016.

Rybczynski, Witold. *Home: A Short History of an Idea*. New York: Penguin Books, 1987.

Sartre, Jean-Paul. *Nausea*. Translated by Lloyd Alexander. New York: New Directions, 2013.

Satrapi, Marjane. *Persepolis: The Story of a Childhood*. New York: Pantheon, 2004.

Saussure, Ferdinand de. *Course in General Linguistics*. Translated by Roy Harris. New York: Bloomsbury Academic, 2013.

Schermbrucker, Ben. "'There's No Remaking Reality': Roth and the Embodied Human Condition in *Everyman*." *Philip Roth Studies* 11, no. 2 (Fall 2015): 39–53.

Schuessler, Jennifer. "'Here,' Richard McGuire's Book, an Exhibition at the Morgan." *New York Times*, September 25, 2014, Books. www.nytimes.com/2014/09/26/books/here-richard-mcguires-book-an-exhibition-at-the-morgan.html.

Scruton, Roger. *Beauty: A Very Short Introduction.* Oxford: Oxford University Press, 2011.

Searle, John R. *The Mystery of Consciousness.* New York: New York Review of Books, 1997.

Seneca, Matt. "Here | The Comics Journal." Accessed June 2, 2017. www.tcj.com/reviews/here/.

Shechner, Mark. *Up Society's Ass, Copper: Rereading Philip Roth.* Madison: University of Wisconsin Press, 2003.

Siegel, Daniel J. *Pocket Guide to Interpersonal Neurobiology: An Integrative Handbook of the Mind.* New York: W. W. Norton, 2012.

Sitter, Deborah Ayer. "The Making of a Man: Dialogic Meaning in *Beloved.*" *African American Review* 26, no. 1 (Spring 1992): 17–29.

Sokolowski, Robert. *Phenomenology of the Human Person.* Cambridge: Cambridge University Press, 2008.

Solomon, Barbara H. *Critical Essays on Toni Morrison's "Beloved."* New York: Twayne Publishers, 1998.

Spaemann, Robert. *Love and the Dignity of Human Life: On Nature and Natural Law.* Foreword by David L. Schindler. Grand Rapids, MI: Eerdmans, 2012.

———. *Persons: The Difference between "Someone" and "Something."* Oxford: Oxford University Press, 2006.

Steiner, George. *Grammars of Creation.* London: Faber & Faber, 2001.

Taliaferro, Charles. *The Golden Cord: A Short Book on the Secular and the Sacred.* 1st ed. Notre Dame, IN: University of Notre Dame Press, 2012.

Taylor, Charles. *The Language Animal: The Full Shape of the Human Linguistic Capacity.* Cambridge, MA: Belknap Press of Harvard University Press, 2016.

———. *A Secular Age.* Cambridge, MA: Belknap Press of Harvard University Press, 2007.

———. *Sources of the Self: The Making of the Modern Identity.* Cambridge, MA: Harvard University Press, 1989.

"The Proprietary House." Accessed June 2, 2017. www.theproprietaryhouse.org.

Tomasello, Michael. *Constructing a Language: A Usage-Based Theory of Language Acquisition.* Cambridge, MA: Harvard University Press, 2005.

Turner, Mark. *The Literary Mind: The Origins of Thought and Language.* Rev. ed. New York: Oxford University Press, 1998.

Vanhoozer, Kevin J., Craig G. Bartholomew, Daniel J. Treier, and N. T. Wright, eds. *Dictionary for Theological Interpretation of the Bible.* London: Baker Academic, 2005.

Vernant, Jean-Pierre. "One . . . Two . . . Three: Eros." In *Before Sexuality: The Construction of Erotic Experience in the Ancient Greek World.* Princeton, NJ: Princeton University Press, 1990.

Wallace, David Foster. "John Updike, Champion Literary Phallocrat, Drops One; Is This Finally the End for Magnificent Narcissists?" *Observer* (blog). Accessed July 9, 2015. http://observer.com/1997/10/john-updike-champion -literary-phallocrat-drops-one-is-this-finally-the-end-for-magnificent -narcissists/.

Ward, Graham. "How Literature Resists Secularity." *Literature and Theology* 24, no. 1 (2010): 73–88.

Watt, Ian. *The Rise of the Novel*. Berkeley: University of California Press, 1964.

Welker, Michael, ed. *The Depth of the Human Person: A Multidisciplinary Approach*. Grand Rapids, MI: Eerdmans, 2014.

Williams, Rowan. *Grace and Necessity: Reflections on Art and Love*. Harrisburg, PA: Bloomsbury Academic, 2006.

Wilson, Edward O. *Sociobiology: The New Synthesis*. Cambridge, MA: Belknap Press of Harvard University Press, 2000.

Wolf, Maryanne. *Proust and the Squid: The Story and Science of the Reading Brain*. New York: Harper Perennial, 2008.

Wood, James. *The Fun Stuff: And Other Essays*. New York: Farrar, Straus and Giroux, 2012.

Zak, P.J. "Why Inspiring Stories Make Us React: The Neuroscience of Narrative." *Cerebrum: The Dana Forum on Brain Science*. www.dana.org /Cerebrum/2015/Why_Inspiring.

Zimmermann, Jens. *Incarnational Humanism: A Philosophy of Culture for the Church in the World*. Downers Grove, IL: IVP Academic, 2012.

———. "'Quo Vadis'?: Literary Theory beyond Postmodernism." *Christianity & Literature* 53, no. 4 (Summer 2004): 495–519.

Zizioulas, John D. *Being as Communion: Studies in Personhood and the Church*. Crestwood, NY: St. Vladimirs Seminary Press, 1997.

Zunshine, Lisa. *Why We Read Fiction: Theory of Mind and the Novel*. Columbus: Ohio State University Press, 2006.

CHRISTINA BIEBER LAKE is the Clyde S. Kilby Professor of English at Wheaton College. She is the author of a number of books, including *Prophets of the Posthuman: American Fiction, Biotechnology, and the Ethics of Personhood* (University of Notre Dame Press, 2013), and winner of the Aldersgate Prize and the Catholic Press Association Book Award for Faith and Science.

www.ingramcontent.com/pod-product-compliance
Lightning Source LLC
Chambersburg PA
CBHW070927150426
42812CB00049B/1552